OPERATION ICEBERG

1945 VICTORY ON OKINAWA

DANIEL WRINN

CONTENTS

Get your FREE copy of WW2: Spies, Snipers and the World at War	v
Seizing Shuri Castle	1
Operation Iceberg	9
Japanese Defenses	19
Land the Landing Force	23
Battle of Yae Take	31
Typhoon of Steel	37
Situation at Sea	43
Blowtorch and Corkscrew	53
Sugar Loaf Hill	63
Day and Bertoli	69
Screaming Mimi	77
Wrapping up the Fight	85
General Roy Geiger	95
General Pedro del Valle	99
General Lemuel Shepherd Jr.	103
General Francis Mulcahy	105
Blood and Iron	107
US Army Troops	111
Marines Aviation Units	115
Artillery on Okinawa	119
Sherman M-4 Tanks	123
Amphibious Reconnaissance	127
Legacy of Okinawa	131
Also By Daniel Wrinn	137
References	145
About the Author	147

GET YOUR FREE COPY OF WW2: SPIES, SNIPERS AND THE WORLD AT WAR

Never miss a new release by signing up for my free readers group. You'll also get WW2: Spies, Snipers and Tales of the World at War delivered to your inbox. (You can unsubscribe at any time.) Tap here to sign up

SEIZING SHURI CASTLE

At dawn on May 29, 1945, the 1st Marine Division began their fifth consecutive week of frontal assaults. This was part of the Tenth Army's relentless offensive against Japanese defenses in southern Okinawa.

Operation Iceberg's mission to secure Okinawa was now two months old and badly bogged down. The fast-paced opening had been replaced by weeks of exhausting and bloody attrition warfare against the Shuri Castle.

The 1st Division were hemmed in between two other divisions. They had precious little room to maneuver and had advanced less than a thousand yards in eighteen days. An average of fifty-five murderous yards per day. Their sector was one bristling, honeycombed ridgeline after another—Kakazu, Dakeshi, and Wana.

But just beyond was the long shoulder of Shuri Ridge. Nerve center of the Imperial Japanese *Thirty-second Army*. The outpost of dozens of forward artillery observers, who'd made life miserable for the Allied landing force. On this wet, rainy, and cold morning, things were different. It was quieter. After days of savage and bitter fighting, Allied forces overran Conical Hill to the east and Sugar Loaf to the west. Shuri Castle no longer seemed invincible.

The 1/5 Marines moved out cautiously and expected the usual firestorm of enemy artillery at any moment. But there was none. Marines reached the crest of Shuri Ridge without a fight. Amazed, the company commander looked west along the road toward the ruins of Shuri Castle: a medieval fortress of ancient Ryukyuan kings.

Soldiers in the Tenth Army expected the Japanese to defend Shuri to the death, but the place seemed lightly held. Spiteful small arms fire came from nothing more than a rearguard. Field radios buzzed with this surprising news. Shuri Castle laid in the distance, ready for the taking. Marines asked for permission to seize their long-awaited prize.

General Pedro del Valle, CO of the 1st Marine Division,

didn't hesitate. According to corps division boundaries, Shuri Castle belonged to soldiers of the 77th Infantry Division. General del Valle knew his counterpart, Army General Andrew Bruce, would be furious if the Marines snatched their long-sought trophy before his soldiers could arrive. This was a unique opportunity to grab the Tenth Army's primary objective. General del Valle gave the go-ahead, and with that, the 1/5 Marines raced along the west ridge against light opposition and secured Shuri Castle.

After General del Valle's staff did some fancy footwork to keep peace with their army neighbors, they learned the 77th had scheduled a massive castle bombardment that morning. Frantic radio calls averted the near-catastrophe just in time. General Bruce was infuriated by the Marines' unauthorized initiative. Del Valle later wrote: "I don't think a single Army commander would talk to me after that."

Through the inter-service aggravation, Allied forces had achieved much this morning. For two months, Shuri Castle had provided the Japanese with a superb field of observed fire —covering southern Okinawa's entire five-mile neck. But as the 1/5 Marines deployed into a defensive line within the castle's rubble, they were unaware that a Japanese rearguard still occupied a massive subterranean headquarters underneath them. Marines soon discovered that directly under their muddy boondockers was the underground headquarters of the Japanese *Thirty-second Army*. This mammoth complex was over 1,200 feet long and 160 feet deep: all dug by pick and shovel.

The enemy had stolen a march on the approaching Tenth Army. Japanese forces retreated south during the rains and occupied the third (final) ring of their prepared underground defenses: a series of fortified escarpments on the Kiyamu Peninsula.

Seizing Shuri Castle was an indisputable milestone in the

Okinawa campaign. Still, it was a hollow victory. Like the flag-raising on Iwo Jima's Suribachi signified the end of the beginning of that prolonged battle. The capture of Shuri Castle did not end the fighting. The savage slugfest on Okinawa continued for another twenty-four days—while the plum rains fell and the horrors and dying on both sides continued.

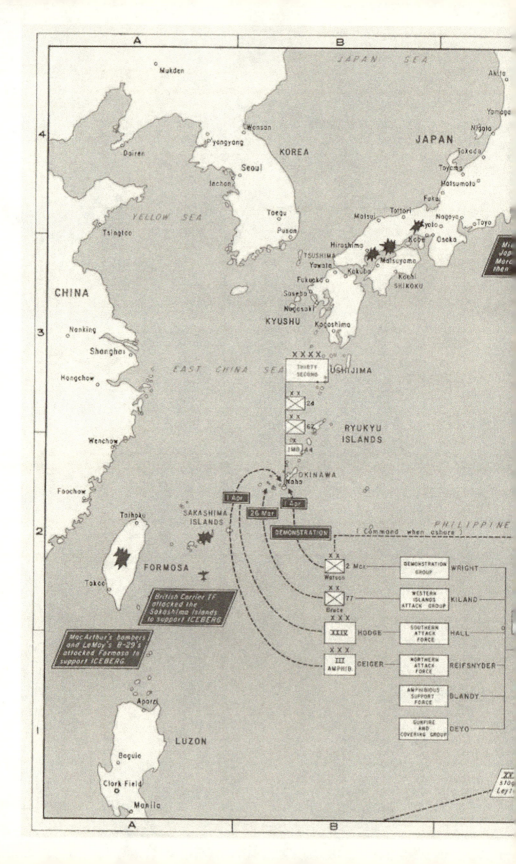

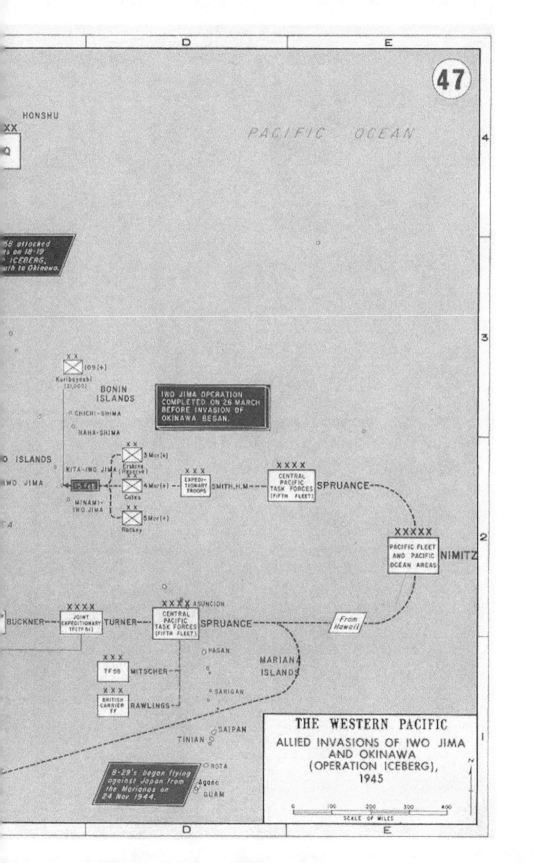

OPERATION ICEBERG

The battle of Okinawa covered a seven-hundred-mile arc from Kyushu to Formosa. It involved a million combatants—Japanese, Americans, British, and Okinawan natives. This battle rivaled the Normandy invasion because it was the biggest and bloodiest operation of the Pacific War. In eighty-two days of combat, Allied forces and unfortunate noncombatants suffered an average of 3,000 lives lost a day.

By the spring of 1945, the Empire of Japan was a wounded wild animal: desperate, cornered, and furious. Japanese leaders knew Okinawa under Allied control would be transformed into "the England of the Pacific." It would serve as a staging point for the invasion of the sacred homeland. The Japanese would sacrifice everything to avoid the unspeakable disgrace of unconditional surrender and foreign occupation.

The US Navy was presented with its greatest operational challenge to date: how to protect a gigantic and exposed amphibious task force tethered to the beachhead against Japanese *kamikaze* attacks. Okinawa would be the ultimate test of US amphibious power and projection. Could Allied forces in the Pacific Theater plan and execute such a massive assault against a heavily defended landmass? Could the Allies integrate the tactical capabilities of all the services and fend off every imaginable form of counterattack while maintaining operational momentum?

Operation Iceberg was not executed in a vacuum. Preparatory action to the invasion kicked off at the same time campaigns on Iwo Jima and the Philippines were still being wrapped up—another strain on Allied resources. But as dramatic and sprawling as the battle of Okinawa proved to be, both sides saw this contest as an example of the even more desperate fighting soon to come with the invasion of the Japanese home islands. The closeness of Okinawa to Japan was well within medium bomber and fighter escort range. Its valuable military ports, anchorages, airfields, and training areas made this skinny island imperative for Allied forces— eclipsing their earlier plans for the seizure of Formosa.

Okinawa is the largest of the Ryukyuan Islands. The island sits at the apex of a triangle nearly equidistant to strategic areas. Formosa is 330 miles to the southwest, Kyushu is 350 miles to the north, while Shanghai is 450 miles to the west. As on so many Pacific battlefields, Okinawa had a peaceful heritage. Officially an administrative prefecture of Japan (forcibly seized in 1879), Okinawans were proud of their long Chinese legacy and unique sense of community.

Imperial headquarters in Tokyo did little to garrison or fortify Okinawa at the beginning of the Pacific War. After the Allies conquered Saipan, Japanese headquarters sent reinforcements and fortification materials to critical areas within the "Inner Strategic Zone," Peleliu, the Philippines, Iwo Jima, and Okinawa.

Imperial Japanese headquarters on Okinawa formed a

new field army: the *Thirty-second Army*. They funneled different trained components from Japan's armed perimeter in China, Manchuria, and the home islands. American submarines took a deadly toll on these Japanese troop movements. On June 29, 1944, the USS *Sturgeon* torpedoed the transport *Toyama Maru*. She sank with a loss of 5,600 troops of the *44th Independent Mixed Brigade* en route for Okinawa. It would take the Japanese the rest of the year to replace that loss.

In October 1944, US Joint Chiefs decided to act on the strategic value of the Ryukyus. They tasked Admiral Nimitz with seizing Okinawa after the Iwo Jima campaign. The Joint Chiefs ordered Nimitz to seize, occupy, and defend Okinawa before transforming the captured island into an advanced staging base for the invasion of Japan.

Nimitz turned to his most veteran commanders to execute this mission. Admiral Spruance, the victor of Midway and the Battle of the Philippine Sea, would command the US Fifth Fleet (debatably the most powerful armada of warships ever assembled). Admiral Kelly Turner, veteran of the Solomons and Central Pacific landings, would command all amphibious forces under Spruance. But Kelly Turner's military counterpart would no longer be the old warhorse General Holland Smith. Iwo Jima was Smith's last fight. Now the expeditionary forces had grown to the size of a field army with 182,000 assault troops. Army General Simon Buckner (son of the Confederate general who fought against Grant at Fort Donaldson in the American Civil War) would command the newly formed US Tenth Army.

General Buckner made sure the Tenth Army reflected his multi-service composition. Thirty-four Marine officers served on Buckner's staff, including General Oliver P. Smith as his deputy Chief of Staff. Smith later wrote: "the Tenth Army became, in effect, a joint task force."

Six veteran divisions, two Marine and four Army, composed Buckner's landing force. A division from each service was marked for reserve duty—another sign of the growth of Allied amphibious power in the Pacific. Earlier in the war, Americans had landed one infantry division on Guadalcanal, two in the Palaus, and three each on Iwo Jima and Saipan. But by spring 1945, Buckner and Spruance could count on eight experienced divisions besides those still on Luzon and Iwo Jima.

The Tenth Army had three major operational components. Army General John Hodge commanded the XXIV Corps, composed of the 77th and 96th Infantry Divisions (with the 27th Infantry Division in floating reserve and the 81st Infantry Division in area reserve). Marine General Roy Geiger commanded the III Amphibious Corps, composed of the 1st and 6th Marine Divisions (with the 2nd Marine Division held in floating reserve). Marine General Francis Mulcahy commanded the Tenth Army's Tactical Air Force and the 2nd Marine Aircraft Wing.

The Marine components for Operation Iceberg were scattered. The 1st Marines had returned from Peleliu to "Pitiful Pavuvu" in the Russell Islands to prepare for the next fight. The 1st Marine Division had been the first to deploy into the Pacific. They executed brutal amphibious campaigns on Guadalcanal, Cape Gloucester, and Peleliu. Over one-third of the 1st Marines were veterans of two of those battles.

Pavuvu's tiny island limited work-up training, but a large-scale exercise on neighboring Guadalcanal enabled the division to integrate its replacements and returning veterans. General del Valle drilled his Marines in tank-infantry training under the protective umbrella of supporting howitzer fire.

The 6th Marine Division was the only division formed overseas in the war. General Lemuel Shepherd activated the colors and assumed command on September 12, 1944. While this unit was newly formed, it was not green—several former Marine Raiders with combat experience comprised the heart of this Marine division. General Shepherd used his time and the more extensive facilities on Guadalcanal to conduct work-up training from the platoon to the regimental level. He looked ahead to Okinawa and emphasized rapid troop deployments and large-scale operations in built-up combat areas.

General LeRoy Hunt commanded the 2nd Marine Division. Hunt's Marines had returned to Saipan after the conquest of Tinian. The division had absorbed 8,000 replacements and trained for a wide-ranging series of mission assignments as a strategic reserve. The 2nd Division possessed a vital lineage in the Pacific War at Guadalcanal, Tarawa, Saipan, and Tinian. Its presence in the Ryukyus' waters would establish a fearsome "amphibious force-in-being" to distract the Japanese on Okinawa. This division would pay an unequal price for its bridesmaid role in the coming campaign.

The Marine assault force preparing for Okinawa was dealt another organizational change—the fourth of the war. Marine headquarters constantly reviewed "lessons learned" in the war and had just completed a series of revisions to the table of organization for its divisions and components. While it would not become official until a month after the landing, the divisions had already made most changes.

The overall size of each division increased to 19,176 (from 17,465). This was done by adding an assault signal company, a rocket platoon (Buck Rogers Men), a fifty-five man assault platoon in each regimental headquarters, and a war dog platoon. Motor transport, artillery, and service units also received slight increases, as did machine-gun platoons in each rifle company. But the most timely weapons change happened by replacing the 75mm half-tracks with the new M-7s (105mm self-propelled howitzer). Artillery regiment purists did not approve of these weapons being deployed by the infantry. These M-7s would not be used as massed howitzers but as direct fire "siege guns" against the thousands of fortified caves on Okinawa.

Marine Corps Headquarters backed up these last-minute changes by providing the required replacements to land the assault divisions at full strength. Sometimes the skills required did not match. Some artillery regiments absorbed a flood of radar technicians and anti-aircraft artillery gunners from old defense battalions. But the manpower and equipment shortfalls that had plagued earlier operations were overcome by the time the assault force embarked on Operation Iceberg.

Even this late in the war, operational intelligence was unsatisfactory before the landing. At Tarawa and Tinian, the pre-assault combat intelligence had been brilliant. But at Okinawa, the landing force did not have accurate figures of the enemy's weapons or abilities.

The cloud cover over the island prevented accurate and complete photo-reconnaissance. Also, the ingenuity of the Japanese commander and the extraordinary digging skills of the enemy garrison helped disguise the island's true defenses.

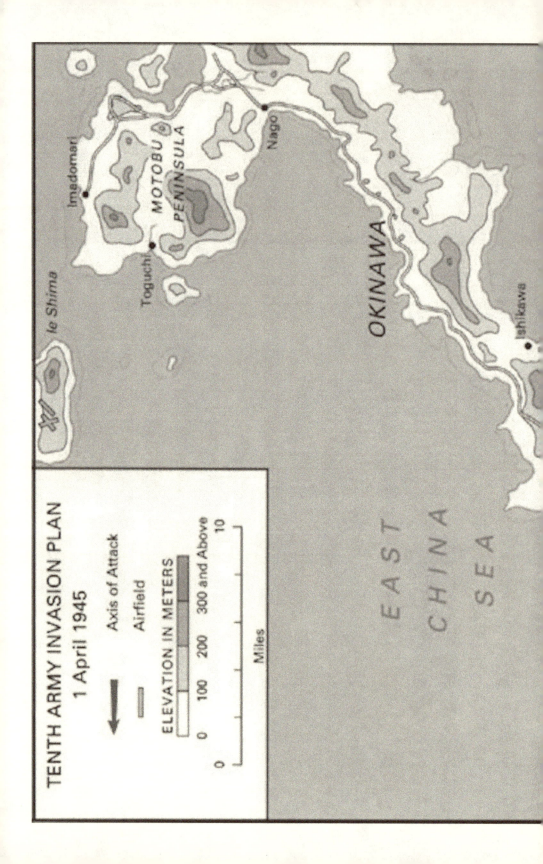

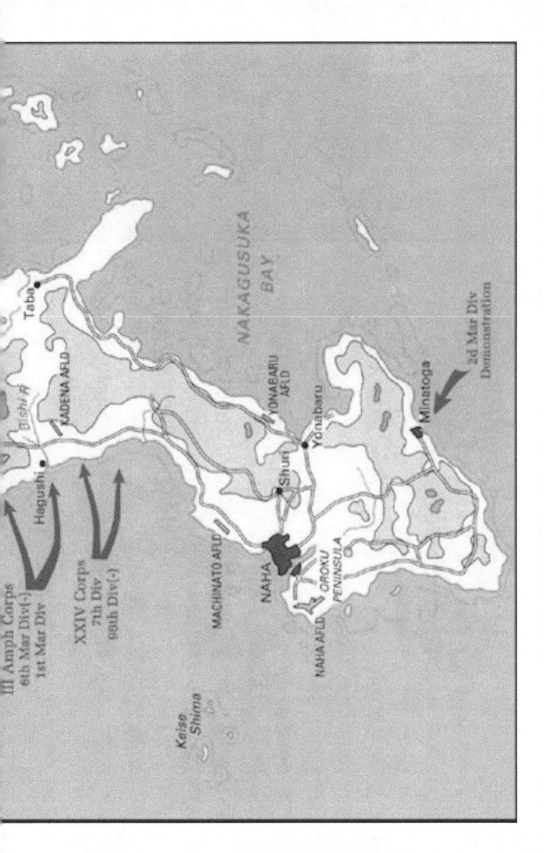

JAPANESE DEFENSES

Okinawa is sixty miles long, but only the lower third of the island had the military objectives of anchorages, ports, and airfields. In August 1944. Japanese General Mitsuru Ushijima took command of the *Thirty-second Army*. He understood the fight would be fought in the south and concentrated his forces there.

He decided to not challenge the probable Allied landings in Hagushi along the broad beaches of the southwest coast. He believed that doing so would lose him the Kadena and Yontan Airfields. This decision allowed him to conserve his forces and fight the only battle that stood a chance: an in-depth defense, underground and protected from the overpowering Allied air and arms superiority.

This clash of cave warfare and attrition would be like the recent battles on Peleliu and Iwo Jima. Each had taken a terrifying cost to Allied invaders. General Ushijima sought to replicate this strategy. He would go underground and sting the Allies with high caliber gunfire from his freshly excavated fireport caves. He believed by bleeding the landing force and bogging down their momentum, he could buy the Imperial Army and Navy's air arms enough time to destroy the fifth fleet with massed *kamikaze* attacks.

General Ushijima had 100,000 Imperial troops on the island, including thousands of Okinawan Home Guard (conscripts known as *Boeitai)*. He had a disproportionate number of heavy weapons and artillery in his command. The Allies in the Pacific would not encounter a more formidable concentration of 47mm antitank guns, 320mm spigot mortars, 120mm mortars, and 150mm howitzers. The strategic decision to invade Peleliu, Iwo Jima, and the Philippines before Okinawa gave the enemy seven months to develop their defenses.

Allied forces had already seen what the Japanese could do to fortify a position in a short time. On Okinawa they achieved stunning success. They worked almost exclusively with hand tools: not one bulldozer on the entire island. The Japanese dug miles of underground fighting positions and honeycombed southern Okinawa's ridges and draws. They stocked each position with reserves of food, water, ammunition, and medical supplies. Allied forces anticipated a fierce defense of the southwestern beaches and the airfields, followed by a general counterattack. Then, the battle would be over except for some mop-up and light patrolling.

The Allies could not have been more mistaken.

The assault plan called for the advance seizure of the Kerama Retto Islands after several days of preparatory air and naval bombardment. Followed by a massive four-division assault on the Hagushi Beaches. During the primary assault, the 2nd Marine Division, with a separate naval task force, would duplicate the assault on Okinawa's southeast coast (Minatoga Beaches).

Love-Day (chosen to avoid planning confusion with D-Day being planned for Iwo Jima) would happen on April 1, 1945.

Operation Iceberg

Hardly anyone failed to remark about the irony of April Fool's Day and Easter Sunday.

The US Fifth Fleet was a breathtaking sight as it steamed toward the Ryukyus. Marines who'd returned to the Pacific from the original amphibious offensive on Guadalcanal thirty-one months earlier gaped at the quantity of landing craft in the assault ships. The armada stretched to the horizon—a genuinely incredible, mind-boggling vista.

*　*　*

On March 26, the 77th Infantry Division skillfully secured Kerama Retto. A move that surprised the Japanese and generated enormous operational dividends. Admiral Turner now had a series of sheltered anchorages to repair ships likely to be damaged by *kamikaze* attacks. Soldiers discovered stockpiled Japanese suicide boats—over 300 powerboats equipped with high explosive rams to sink the thin-skinned troop transports.

Major James Jones commanded the Force Reconnaissance Battalion. His battalion paved the way before each landing with stealthy scouting missions the night before. Jones' recon Marines scouted and found the barren sand spits of Keise Shima undefended. After reporting that welcome news, the Army landed a battery of 155mm "Long Toms" on the small inlets, adding to their significant firepower and the naval bombardment of Okinawa's southwest coast.

Admiral Turner's minesweepers cleared approaches to the southwestern beaches. Navy frogmen and Marines detonated hundreds of man-made obstacles. After seven days of preliminary bombardment, Allied ships fired over 25,000 rounds of 5-inch shells. This shelling produced more of a spectacle than a destructive effect. The Allied forces believed General Ushijima's troops would be arrayed around the beaches and airfields.

While that scale and duration of bombardment would've saved many lives on Iwo Jima: on Okinawa, this precious ordinance was largely wasted and produced few results.

Tensions were high in landing force transports. The 60mm mortar section of Company K, 3/5 Marines learned that the casualty rates on Love-Day were estimated to reach 85%. According to Private First Class Eugene Sledge: "this is not conducive to a good night's sleep."

A Japanese soldier observing the massive armada bearing down on Okinawa wrote in his diary: "it's like a frog meeting a snake and waiting for the snake to eat him."

LAND THE LANDING FORCE

The Allied invasion got off to a roaring start. The few enemy defenders still in the area at dawn on April 1 immediately agreed with the wisdom of conceding the beaches to the landing force.

The massive armada gathered from ports all over the Pacific now bore down on Okinawa's southwest coast: ready to deploy a 182,000-man landing force onto the beach. The ultimate forcible entry—the embodiment of all painfully learned amphibious lessons from the crude beginnings at Guadalcanal and North Africa.

Admiral Turner made his final review of the weather conditions in the objective area. As at Iwo Jima, the amphibious assault was fortunate to have good weather for the critical initial landing. Skies were clear, winds and surf were moderate. The temperature was 75 degrees.

At 0406, Turner ordered: "Land the landing force." That phrase set off a sequential countdown to the first assault waves smashing into the beaches at H-hour. Combat troops crowded the rails of the transports to witness an extraordinary display of Allied naval power. A sustained bombardment by rockets and shells from hundreds of ships. Formations of Allied attack aircraft streaked low over the beaches: strafing and bombing at will. Japanese fire was ineffective and scattered, even against this massive armada assembled offshore.

The diversionary force carrying the 2nd Marine Division set out to bait the Japanese with a feint landing on the opposite coast. This amphibious force steamed into position and launched amphibian tractors and Higgins boats loaded with combat Marines in seven waves toward Minatoga Beach. The fourth wave commander paid careful attention to the clock and crossed the line of departure at exactly 0830—the time of the actual H-hour assault on the western coast. Then, the Higgins boats and LVTs turned away and returned to the transports: mission accomplished.

The diversionary landing achieved its purpose. General Ushijima had placed several front-line infantry and artillery units in the Minatoga Beach area for several weeks as a contingency against an expected secondary landing. His officers reported to Imperial headquarters on Love-Day morning: "enemy landing attempt on east coast blocked with heavy enemy losses."

This deception came at a high cost. *Kamikaze* pilots were convinced this was the main assault. They came in waves and struck the small force that morning, damaging the troopships *LST 844* and *Hinsdale*. The 3/2 Marines and the 2nd Amphibian Tractor Battalion suffered fifty casualties. The troopships lost an equal number of sailors. Ironically, the division that was expected to have the most minor damage or casualties in the battle lost more men than any other division in the Tenth Army that day. According to Operation Officer Colonel Sam Taxis: "we'd requested air cover for the feint but were told the threat was 'incidental.'"

In the southwest, the main assault force faced little resistance. A massive coral reef provided an offshore barrier to the beaches on Hagushi. But by early evening, the reef no longer presented a threat to the landing force. Unlike on Tarawa, where the reef dominated the tactical progress of the battle. General Buckner had over 1,400 LVTs to transport the assault waves from ship to shore without delay.

Eight miles of LVTs churned across the line of departure just behind 360 armored LVT-As that blasted away at the beach with their snub-nosed 75mm howitzers as they advanced the final four thousand yards. Behind the LVTs were 750 amphibious trucks with the first of the direct support artillery battalions. The horizon behind the amphibious trucks was filled with lines of landing boats. They paused at the reef to marry with the outbound LVTs. Marines and soldiers had exhaustively rehearsed transfer line operations—there was no pause in the assault momentum.

The Bisha Gawa river mouth marked the boundary

between IIIAC and XXIV Corps along the Hagushi beaches. The tactical plan called for the two divisions to land abreast—the 6th on the left and the 1st on the right. The endless rehearsal of thousands of hours paid off. The initial assault touched down at 0830: the designated H-hour. Marines stormed out of their LVTs, swarming over the sea walls and berms into the great unknown. The Okinawa invasion had begun. Within the first hour, the Tenth Army had over 16,000 combat troops ashore.

Despite the dire intelligent predictions and their own combat experience, the troops' landing was a cakewalk—almost unopposed. Private First Class Eugene Sledge's mortar section began singing "Little Brown Jug" at the top of their lungs. He later wrote how he couldn't believe his good luck: "I didn't hear a single shot all morning. It was unbelievable."

Many Marine veterans expected enemy fire at any second. Later that day, General del Valle's LVT got stuck in a pothole en route to the beach. "It was the worst twenty minutes I'd ever spent in my life," the general later wrote.

That morning continued to deliver pleasant surprises to the assault force. No mines along the beaches, the main bridge over the Bishi River was still intact, and both airfields were lightly defended. Marines took Yontan Airfield at 1300 while soldiers from the 7th Infantry Division had no problem securing nearby Kadena.

After securing the assault beaches, the landing force left plenty of room for the follow-on forces. Division commanders accelerated the landing of artillery battalions, tanks, and reserves. This massive buildup was hampered by a few glitches. Four artillery pieces went down when their amphibious trucks foundered along the reef. Several other Sherman tanks grounded on the reef. The 3/1 Marines arrived at the transfer line by 1800 but spent an uncomfortable night in their boats because enough LVTs were not available for the last leg at that hour. While only minor inconveniences, by the day's end, the Tenth Army had 60,000 troops ashore and occupied an expanded beach eight miles long and two miles deep.

The landing was not bloodless. Snipers wounded Major John Gustafson, CO of the 3/5 Marines, later that afternoon. Other men went down to enemy mortars and machine-gun fire. But the Tenth Army's entire losses (including the hard-luck 2nd Division) were 159 casualties with twenty-eight killed.

This was less than ten percent of casualties suffered by V Amphibious Corps on the first bloody day of Iwo Jima.

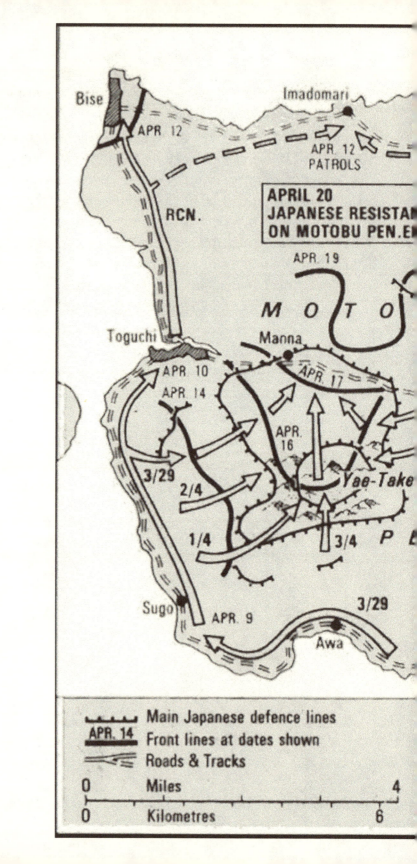

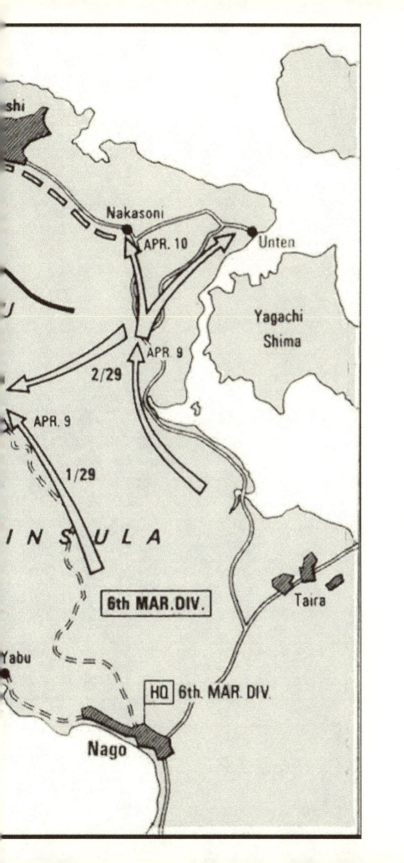

BATTLE OF YAE TAKE

The assault force's momentum did not slow down after the Tenth Army broke out of the beachhead. The 7th Infantry reached the east coast on the second day. On the third day, the 1st Marine Division secured the Katchin Peninsula and cut the island in two. By now, elements of the III Amphibious Corps had reached their objective initially thought to require eleven days. Colonel Victor Krulak, 6th Marine Division operations officer, recalled General Shepherd's orders: "Plow ahead as fast as you can. The Japs are on the run."

Krulak thought: *Well hell, we didn't have them on the run. They weren't there.*

The 6th Division swung north, while the 1st Marine Division moved to the northwest—their immediate problems stemming not from the enemy but a slow supply system still processing on the beach. The reef-side transfer line worked well for troops but not for cargo.

Navy Seabees worked to build a causeway for the reef. At the same time, the 1st Division demonstrated their amphibious know-how learned on Peleliu. They mounted swinging cranes on powered causeways and secured craft to the seaward side of the reef. When boats pulled alongside, cranes lifted nets filled with combat cargo into open hatches of waiting LVTs and amphibious trucks. This worked so well that the division divided its assets within the Tenth Army.

Beach congestion slowed the logistical process. Both Marine divisions used their replacements as shore party teams. Inexperience combined with a constant call for new replacements caused traffic control problems in establishing functional supply dumps and pilferage. This was not new. Other divisions in earlier operations had had the same problems. The quickly advancing divisions desperately needed bulk fuel and motor transport—but these were slow to land and distribute.

The undeveloped road network on Okinawa made this problem worse. Colonel Ed Snedeker, CO of the 7th Regiment in the 1st Marine Division, wrote: "The movement from the west coast landing beaches on Okinawa across the island was difficult because of the rugged terrain. It was physically exhausting for personnel to be on the transports for such a long time. This also presented an initial impossible supply problem in the Seventh's zone of action because of the lack of roads."

General Mulcahy brought the Tactical Air Force command post ashore on L+1. Operating out of crude quarters between Kadena and Yontan Airfields, Mulcahy closely watched the Seabees and Army-Marine engineers progress repairing the captured airfields. A Marine observation plane was the first Allied aircraft to land on April 2. Two days later, the airfields were ready to accept fighters. By the eighth day, General Mulcahy could accommodate medium bombers and assumed control of all ashore fleet aircraft.

Mulcahy's fighter arm, the Air Defense Command, was established on shore under the command of Marine General

William Wallace. Graceful F4U Corsairs of Marine Aircraft Group (MAG 31) flew in from escort carriers. Wallace tasked them with flying combat air patrols over the fleet to tackle the vicious mass of *kamikaze* attacks plaguing the fleet. Most Marine fighter pilots' initial missions were combat air patrols, while (ironically) Navy squadrons on board escort carriers handled the close air support jobs.

At dawn, Marine Corsairs took off from the airfields and flew combat air patrols over the far-flung fifth fleet. They passed Navy Hellcats coming in from the fleet to support the Marines fighting on the ground. Other air units poured into the two Army airfields: night fighters, torpedo bombers, and an Army Air Forces fighter wing. The Okinawan airfields were not safe-havens. They received nightly artillery fire from long-range bombing the entire first month ashore. But the two airfields remained in operation around the clock. They were an invaluable asset in support of Operation Iceberg.

* * *

General Roy Geiger unleashed the 6th Marine Division to sweep north while the 1st Division hunted down and destroyed small bands of enemy guerrillas in the center of the island. Riflemen rode topside on tanks and self-propelled guns streaming northward against the fleeing enemy. Not since Tinian did Marines enjoy such invigorating mobility. On April 7, Marines seized Nagano, the largest town in northern Okinawa. The Navy swept for mines and deployed Underwater Demolition Teams to breach obstacles and open the port for direct seaborne delivery of crucial supplies.

Corporal James Day with the 22nd Marines was impressed at the momentum of the operation. He wrote: "Hell, here we are in Nago. It wasn't tough at all. Up until that time, our squad hadn't lost a man." The 22nd Marines continued north through a rugged and broken country. They reached Hedo Misaki at the far end of the island on L +12 after advancing fifty-five miles from the landing beaches at Hagushi.

The honeymoon was coming to a swift end for the rest of the 6th Division. Northwest of Nago, on its bulby nose, the Motobu Peninsula jutted out into the East China Sea. In a six mile area around the 1,200 foot Mount Yae Take, Colonel Takesiko Udo and his *Kunigami Detachment* were in prepared defensive positions. The delaying tactics were over. Udo's force comprised two thousand seasoned troops from the *44th Independent Mixed Brigade*. He had two rifle battalions, a regimental gun company, and an anti-tank company at his disposal.

Mount Yae Take was a defender's dream. Steep vines tangled with dense vegetation. Japanese troops booby-trapped the approaches with mines and mounted 20mm machine cannons and heavier weapons deep inside their caves. According to Colonel Krulak: "They were just there. They weren't going anywhere. They were going to fight to the death. They had a lot of Navy guns that came off disabled ships. They dug them way back in holes where their arc of fire was not more than ten degrees." An artillery battalion of fifteen Marines had the misfortune to lay their guns directly within the narrow arc of a hidden 150mm cannon. "They lost two howitzers before you could spell cat."

The battle of Yae Take was the first real fight for the 6th Marine Division. Five days of difficult and deadly combat against a determined enemy. The 4th and the 29th Marines earned their spurs here. They developed teamwork and tactics, putting them in a good position for the long, bloody campaign ahead.

One aspect of General Shepherd's success in this battle stemmed from his desire to place proven leaders in command of his troops. On the 15th, Shepherd relieved Colonel Victor Bleasdale (a decorated World War I Marine) and installed Guadalcanal veteran Colonel William Whaling as the commanding officer of the 29th Marines. After an enemy sniper killed Major Bernard Greene, commanding the 1/4 Marines, Colonel Alan Shapley assigned his own XO, Colonel Fred Beans (former Marine Raider), as his replacement.

The ferocious fighting continued with three Allied battalions attacking from the west and two from the east. They were protected against friendly fire by the steep pinnacle separating them. Logistics were essential in this fight. Every Marine (from private to general) who climbed that mountain to the front lines carried either a 5-gallon water can or a case of ammo. All hands coming down the mountain helped carry the stretchers of wounded Marines. On April 15, a company of the 2/4 Marines took sixty-five casualties—including three consecutive company commanders.

The next day Marines secured the ridge with the help of the battleship *Tennessee's* 14-inch guns and Marine Corsairs low-level pocket bombing.

Colonel Udo and his troops from the *Kunigami Detachment* died to the last man. On April 20, General Shepherd announced the Motobu Peninsula was secured. His Marines had earned a precious victory, but the cost did not come cheap. The 6th Marine Division suffered 757 wounded and 207 killed in the battle.

In his journal, an impressed General Oliver Smith wrote: "This northern campaign should dispel the belief held by some that Marines are beach-bound and not capable of rapid movement. Our Marines raced over rugged terrain and repaired roads and blown bridges while successfully opening new unloading points. They reached the island's northern tip —over fifty miles away from the landing beaches—in fourteen days. Followed by a seven-day campaign to secure the Motobu Peninsula."

The 77th Infantry Division landed on the island Ie Shima and seized its airfields during the battle for Motobu Peninsula. On April 16, Major Jones' recon Marines paved the way by taking a small islet 6,200 yards offshore called Minna Shima. Here, soldiers positioned a 105mm battery to support onshore operations. The 77th needed plenty of fire support to fight the 5,000 enemy defending the island. The Army soldiers overwhelmed them in six days of hard fighting at the cost of 1,100 casualties.

A popular war correspondent named Ernie Pyle, who'd landed with the Marines on L-Day, was shot in the head by a Japanese sniper. Marines and soldiers alike grieved over Pyle's death just as they'd done six days earlier with the news of FDR's passing.

TYPHOON OF STEEL

The 1st Marine Division fought a different campaign in April than their sister division to the north. They spent their days processing refugees and their nights on ambushes and patrols. Snipers and guerrillas exacted a steady but small toll.

The "Old Breed" Marines welcomed this style of low intensity. After many months in the tropics, they found Okinawa refreshing and rustic. Marines were concerned about the welfare of the thousands of Okinawan refugees streaming in from the heavy fighting.

According to Private First Class Eugene Sledge: "The most pitiful things about the Okinawan civilians were that they were totally bewildered by the shock of our invasion, and they were scared to death of us. Countless times they passed us on the way to the rear with sadness, fear, and confusion on their faces."

Sledge and his companions in the 5th Marines could tell by the sound of the intense artillery fire to the south that the XXIV Corps had smashed into General Ushijima's ring of outer defenses. Inside that first week, soldiers from the 7th and 96th Divisions figured out the riddle: Where the hell are the Japs? By the second week, General Buckner and General Hodge were aware of Ushijima's intentions and the depth and range of his defensive positions.

Along with minefields, caves, and reverse slope emplacements, the Shuri defensive complex contained the most large-caliber weapons the Allies had ever faced in the Pacific. These positions had mutually supporting fires from the adjacent hills and ridgelines—honeycombed with fighting holes and caves. Keeping a strict adherence to these intricate networks of mutually supporting positions required an iron discipline from enemy troops. The enemy's discipline prevailed. Allied forces found themselves entering into savage killing zones.

Japanese tactics along the front were to isolate and contain Allied penetration by grazing fire from supporting positions. Then, they'd overwhelm exposed troops with a storm of preregistered heavy mortar shells while enemy troops swarmed out of their tunnels and counterattacked. Japanese troops often shot down more Allied troops during their extraction from a fire swept hilltop than they did in the initial advance.

General Buckner committed the 27th Infantry Division to the southern front. He had General Geiger loan him his corps artillery and 11th Marines to help beef up fire support. The XXIV Corps now had an additional four 155mm battalions, three 105mm battalions, and one 75mm pack howitzer battalion to add to the underway bombardment of Ushijima's outer defenses. Colonel Fred Henderson took command of a field artillery group composed of a 155mm gun battalion and an eight-inch howitzer battalion (the Henderson Group), which provided massive fire support for the Tenth Army.

It took time to build the adequate units of fire for field artillery battalions to support the mammoth, three-divisional offensive that General Buckner wanted. After a week of inactivity passed along the front, the Japanese made their own adjustments and prepared for the coming offensive.

On L +7 (April 18) General Buckner moved the command post of the Tenth Army onshore, and the new offensive began the following day. It was preceded by a wicked preliminary bombardment (typhoon of steel) of twenty-seven artillery batteries, six hundred aircraft, and eighteen ships. But the enemy just burrowed deeper into their subterranean fortress and waited. They waited for the hellish pounding to stop. They waited for the Allied infantry to advance into their well-designed killing traps.

On April 19, XXIV Corps executed the assault. They made *some* gains before getting thrown back with heavy casualties. The enemy extracted a heavy toll from Allied tanks—particularly those supporting the 27th Infantry Division. The fighting around Kakazu Ridge had separated tanks from supporting infantry by fire, and the Japanese knocked off twenty-two of them with everything from hand-delivered satchel charges to 47mm guns.

This disastrous battle on April 19 gave the Tenth Army a dose of reality. The walk in the sun was over. Overcoming enemy defenses around Shuri would require several divisions, massive firepower, and much more time. General Buckner requested General Geiger give him the 1st Tank Battalion to help the 27th Division along the Machinato-Kakazu lines.

General del Valle was livid and complained to Geiger: "They can have my division, but not piecemeal." Marine tank crews and infantry trained together as a team. The 1st Marine Division had perfected tank-infantry offensive attacks in the crucible on Peleliu. Committing tanks to the Army without trained infantry squads would be catastrophic.

Fortunately, Generals Oliver Smith and Roy Geiger made del Valle's points crystal clear to General Buckner. The Tenth Army commander agreed to refrain from any piecemeal commitments of the Marines. On April 24, he ordered Geiger to designate one division as a Tenth Army reserve and make one regiment in that division ready to move south in less than twelve hours. Geiger gave the mission to the 1st Marine Division, and General del Valle advanced the 1st Marines south.

General Buckner and his senior advisers seriously debated opening a second front with an amphibious landing on the Minatoga Beaches. The bloody fighting on the Shuri front helped him decide. As casualties piled up at a shocking rate, Buckner concentrated all of his resources on one front. On April 27, he assigned the 1st Marine Division to the XXIV Corps. Over the next three days, the division advanced south and relieved the shot-up 27th Infantry Division on the right flank. The 6th Division was ordered to prepare for a similar displacement to the south.

Operation Iceberg

The long battle for the southern highlands of Okinawa was now shifting into gear.

Throughout April and with unparalleled ferociousness, Japanese *kamikazes* punished Fifth Fleet ships supporting the operation. The aerial battles became so intense that the western beaches received a deadly, steady rain of shell fragments from thousands of antiaircraft guns in the fleet. There were no safe havens in this battle.

SITUATION AT SEA

The Japanese strategy to defend Okinawa was to make the most of the nation's shrinking resources and zealous patriotism.

General Ushijima planned to bloody the Allied forces in a lengthy battle of attrition, while the Japanese air forces would savage the Fifth Fleet—tethered to the island to support ground forces. Ushijima's strategy would combine passive ground defense with a violent air offensive. Suicidal *kamikaze* tactics were planned on an unprecedented scale.

By spring of 1945, the Allies understood the enemy's decision to sacrifice planes and pilots in reckless *kamikaze* attacks from their time in the Philippines. Individual suicide attacks by anti-shipping swimmers near Iwo Jima and the "human bullet" anti-tank demolitions on Peleliu were common. Japanese headquarters had escalated these tactics to an overwhelming level at Okinawa. They unleashed their newest weapon: *Operation Kikusui* (floating chrysanthemums) devastating mass suicide airstrikes against the fleet.

While small groups of *kamikazes* struck the fleet nightly and achieved some damage, the worst destruction came from concentrated *Kikusui* raids. The Japanese launched ten separate *Kikusui* attacks during the battle on Okinawa—each with over 350 aircraft. Japanese headquarters coordinated these raids and other tactical surprises, like the sacrificial sortie of the *Yamato* and other formidable counter-attacks. These tactics resulted in a shocking loss of life on both sides.

Kamikaze swarms harassed the Fifth Fleet from the time they entered Ryukyuan waters and throughout the battle. Some senior Navy commanders dismissed the threat—inexperienced pilots and rundown planes launched with insufficient fuel to reach Okinawa. While it was true that many of the 2,377 *kamikaze* pilots did not fulfill their mission, Special Attack

Operation Iceberg

Unit pilots who got through the air and surface screens inflicted a wicked toll on the Fifth Fleet.

At the end of the campaign, the Fifth Fleet had endured thirty-four ships sunk, 360 damaged, and over 9,000 casualties: the worst losses ever sustained in a single battle in the history of the US Navy.

The situation at sea became so devastating that smoke from burning ships and offshore escorts blinded Kadena Airfield and caused four returning combat air patrol planes to crash. As the onslaught continued, Admiral Spruance said: "The suicide plane is an effective weapon which we must not underestimate." Spruance spoke from first-hand experience. *Kamikaze* attacks knocked out his first flagship, the heavy cruiser *Indianapolis*, early in the campaign. Then they damaged his replacement flagship—the battleship *New Mexico* two weeks later.

Enemy pilots attacking the fleet off Okinawa had a new weapon: the *Ohka* (Cherry Blossom) bomb. The Allies called this bomb "Baka" (the Japanese word for foolish). A manned rocket packed with 4,400 pounds of explosives launched at ships from the belly of a twin-engine bomber.

The Ohka bombs were the first antiship guided missiles. They shrieked toward their target at an unheard of speed of 500 knots. This new weapon blew the destroyer *Manert L. Abele* out of the water. But luckily for the Allies, most Ohka's missed their targets—the missiles were too fast for the inexperienced pilots to control in their last seconds of glory.

The ultimate suicide attack was the final sortie of the super battleship *Yamato*. One of the world's last great dreadnoughts. She had 18.1-inch guns that could outrange any US battleship. Imperial headquarters dispatched the *Yamato* on her last mission. A bizarre maneuver with no air cover and only a handful of surface escorts—with enough fuel for a one-way trip.

Her mission was to distract American carriers while the Japanese launched a massive *Kikusui* attack against the rest of the fleet. Afterward, the *Yamato* would beach on the west coast of Okinawa and use her massive guns to shoot up the onshore landing force and the thin-skinned amphibious shipping. This daring plan proved to be a complete failure.

This colossal warship would've terrified the fleet protecting an amphibious beachhead in the early years of the war. But not now. US submarines gave Admiral Spruance early warning of the *Yamato's* departure from Japanese waters. Admiral Mark Mitscher asked Spruance: "Shall I take them or will you?" Mitscher commanded the fast carriers of Task Force 58. While Spruance knew his battleship force was eager to avenge their losses at Pearl Harbor—this was no time for nostalgia.

Spruance signaled: "You take them." And with that, Mitscher's Avengers and Hellcats roared into action. They intercepted the *Yamato* a hundred miles from the beach. They sunk her quickly with torpedoes and bombs. It cost the Allied forces eight planes and twelve pilots.

Another bizarre Japanese suicide mission was more effective. On the evening of May 25, seven enemy transport planes loaded with *Giretsu* (Japanese commandos) approached the Yontan Airfield. Vigilant antiaircraft guns flamed five planes, but the surviving plane made a wheels-up belly landing on the airstrip—discharging troops as she slid in sparks and flames along the long surface. Giretsu commandos destroyed eight planes and damaged twice as many more. They ignited 70,000 gallons of aviation fuel, creating chaos and confusion through the night. Jumpy security troops fired into the shadows and injured more of their own men than the Japanese. It took

Operation Iceberg

twelve hours to hunt down and destroy the enemy commandos.

Admiral Spruance desperately tried to reduce the effectiveness of the *kamikaze* strikes. His fast-attack carriers hit enemy airfields in Formosa and Kyushu repeatedly, but the Japanese were experts at camouflage. Marine landing parties were sent to seize the outlying islands to establish fire direction and early warning outposts. Fighter aircraft from all three services took to the skies to intercept the massed waves of suicidal enemy planes.

Not all of these enemy airstrikes were *kamikazes*. Equal numbers of fighters and bombers attacked Allied targets while guiding in the suicide planes. The Japanese used several of their later model fighters like the Nakajima in death-defying air-to-air duels over hundreds of miles of blue ocean.

The far-reaching fast carriers usually made the first interceptions. While many pilots were from the Navy, the task force included two Marine fighter squadrons on the carriers *Bennington* and *Bunker Hill*. Marine pilot Lieutenant Ken Huntington flew the only Marine Corsair in the attack on the *Yamato*. Huntington swept through heavy antiaircraft fire to deliver a bomb on the battle ship's forward turret. Described by war correspondent Robert Sherrod: "one Marine, one bomb, and one Navy Cross."

Marine pilots from MAGs 31 and 33 flying out of Yontan Airfield provided most combat air patrol missions over the fleet. Under General Mulcahy's command, the combat air patrol missions surged from an initial twelve planes to as many as thirty-two, with another dozen on alert. These missions involved countless hours of patrolling in rough weather spiked by sudden violent encounters from enemy raiders. Marine planes ran a double risk. Battling with Japanese fighters often brought both planes within range of jittery shipboard antiaircraft gunners—who sometimes shot down both planes.

On April 16, Marine Corsairs raced to help the picket ship *Laffey* under attack from five *kamikaze* planes. Allied aircraft shot down seventeen enemy planes. Only one Corsair was lost in the fight while chasing an enemy *kamikaze* so low that they both clipped the ship's superstructure and crashed.

Major George Axtell and his "Death Rattlers" (VMF-323) intercepted a large flight of enemy raiders approaching the fleet at dusk. Three Marine pilots shot down sixteen enemy planes in twenty minutes. Major Axtell, the squadron commander, shot down five and became an instant ace. He later described these dog fights: "You'd be flying in and out of clouds and heavy rain. Friendly and enemy aircraft would wind up in a big melee. You'd just keep turning into any enemy aircraft that appeared. It was fast and furious, and the engagement would be over within thirty minutes."

Despite the brave efforts of pilots and ground crews, a few *kamikazes* always got through. Kerama Retto's protected anchorage resembled a floating graveyard of severely damaged ships. The small groups of suicide pilots who appeared every night in the fleet were especially vulnerable during the full moon. A naval officer described the nighttime raids as "witches on broomsticks." The main victims of these nocturnal attacks were the "small boys," amphibs and picket ships.

Nick Floros was a 19-year-old signalman who manned a 20mm gun on the tiny *LSM-120*. One moonless night a *kamikaze* appeared out of nowhere. She glided in, cut her engine off, looking like a giant bat. The Japanese plane smashed into the LCM with a horrific explosion before anyone could fire a shot. While the small LSM loaded with landing force supplies somehow survived the fiery blast, she was immediately towed to Kerama Retto's "demolition yard."

* * *

Japanese headquarters believed the exaggerated claims that the *Kikusui* attacks had crippled the US fleet. Wishful thinking. While the Fifth Fleet may have been battered and bruised by the *kamikaze* onslaught, they were too massive of a force to deter. The fleet endured the worst of these endless air attacks. They never wavered from their primary mission of supporting Okinawa's amphibious assault.

Naval gunfire support had never been so effective. Over 4,000 tons of munitions were delivered on L-Day. Frontline regiments received direct support from a "call-fire" ship and one illumination ship throughout the campaign. The quantity and quality of naval gunfire was summed up in this message from General Shepherd: "The effectiveness of our naval gunfire support was measured by the large number of Japanese encountered. Dead ones."

Even through the most intense *Kikusui* attacks in early April, the fleet still unloaded over half a million tons of supplies onto Hagushi's beaches to support the Tenth Army. They opened the port of Nago by clearing mines and obstacles under fire. The only direct consequence from the massed *kamikaze* attacks was the April 6 sinking of ammunition ships *Hobbs Victory* and *Logan Victory*. This caused a shortage of 155mm artillery and delayed General Buckner's first offensive against Shuri by three days. But the Fifth Fleet deserved its nickname "The fleet that came to stay."

But as April dragged into May, the Tenth Army was bogged down because of lackluster frontal assaults along the Shuri line. Admiral Spruance pressured General Buckner to speed up his attack to reduce the fleet's vulnerability. Nimitz was concerned and flew to Okinawa to "counsel" Buckner. Nimitz said: "we're losing a ship and a half each day we're out here. You gotta get this thing moving."

Senior Marine commanders urged Buckner to play the "amphib card" and execute a massive landing on the southeast coast to turn the enemy's right flank. Several Army generals agreed with this recommendation and mentioned that continuing to assault Shuri with frontal assaults was like putting forces through a meatgrinder.

General Vandegrift, Commandant of the Marine Corps, visited the island and seconded the recommendations given to Buckner. Vandegrift pointed out that Buckner still controlled the 2nd Marines. This veteran amphibious outfit had already demonstrated its capability against the Minatoga Beaches on L-Day. Buckner had sent the 2nd Marine Division to Saipan to reduce their vulnerability from *kamikaze* attacks. But the 2nd Division still had combat-loaded ships at hand and could have opened a second front in Okinawa within days.

General Buckner was a capable and popular commander, but his experience with amphibious warfare was limited. His staff warned of a potential logistical nightmare in opening a second front. His intelligence predicted stiff resistance around the Minatoga beachhead. Buckner knew the high cost of the bloody Anzio operation and the consequences of an amphibious landing far from the main effort. Buckner believed the defenses on Shuri would soon crack under a coordinated application of his massive infantry firepower. Buckner rejected the amphibious option. Admirals' Nimitz and Sherman agreed. But not Admirals Turner and Spruance or the Marines.

Spruance wrote in a private letter: "There are times when I was impatient for some of Holland Smith's drive." And

Operation Iceberg

General Shepherd stated: "General Buckner did not cotton to amphibious operations."

Even Colonel Yahara of the *Thirty-second Army*, conceded later under interrogation that he'd been puzzled by the adherence to a wholly frontal assault from north to south: "The absence of a landing in the south puzzled the *Thirty-second Army*. Especially after the beginning of May, when it was impossible to put up anything more than a token resistance in the south."

But by then, the 2nd Marine Division was feeling like a yo-yo preparing for their assigned missions. Colonel Samuel Taxis had sharp words after the war about Buckner's decision. "I will always feel that the Tenth Army should've been prepared the instant they were found bogged down. They should've thrown a left hook down there in the southern beaches. They had one hell of a powerful reinforced division down there—trained to a gnat's whisker."

General Buckner stood by his decision. There was to be no "left hook." Instead, both the 1st and 6th Divisions joined in the Shuri offensive as infantry divisions under the Tenth Army, and the 2nd Division would remain in Saipan.

BLOWTORCH AND CORKSCREW

According to the Tenth Army's after-action report: "Japanese defensive efforts and continued development and improvement of cave warfare was the most outstanding feature of enemy tactics on Okinawa."

General Ushijima selected the best terrain to defend the Shuri highlands across the southern neck of the island. His troops dominated two of Okinawa's strategic features: the sheltered anchorage of Nakagusuku bay (later called Buckner Bay) to the east, and the port of Naha to the west. Because of this, Allied troops would have to force their way into the enemy's preregistered killing zones to secure their objectives.

Everything about the terrain favored the defenders. The elaborate topography of ridges, draws, and escarpments grouped the battlefield into sections of small unit firefights. The lack of dense vegetation gave the Japanese troops full, interlocking fire and observation from immediate strong points.

Like Iwo Jima, the enemy fought primarily from underground positions to counteract the Allied supremacy in supporting arms. The enemy modified thousands of concrete Okinawa tombs to use as combat outposts. While there were blind spots in the defenses, finding and exploiting them was costly in time and blood.

The most savage fighting of the campaign took place on a compressed battlefield. The distance from Yonabaru on the east coast to the Asa River bridge on the other side of the island was only 9,000 yards. General Buckner advanced abreast with two Army divisions. By May 8, he'd doubled his force by adding two Marine divisions from IIIAC and sent them west. His two XXIV Corps Army Divisions were sent east. Each of these divisions fought brutal, bloody battles against disciplined enemy soldiers defending entrenched and fortified terrain.

By rejecting the amphibious flanking plan in late April, Buckner had fresh divisions ready to deploy and join the general offensive against Shuri. The 77th relieved the 96th in the center, and the 1st Marine Division relieved the 27th Infantry in the west. Colonel Ken Chappell's 1st Marines entered the lines on April 30 and took heavy fire the moment they approached. When the 5th Marines arrived to supplement the relief, enemy gunners were pounding anything that moved.

PFC Eugene Sledge later wrote: "It was hell in there. We raced across an open field with Jap shells screaming and roaring around us with increasing frequency. The thunder and crash of explosions was a nightmare. I was terribly afraid."

General del Valle took command of the western zone on May 1 at 1400. He issued orders for a major assault the following morning. That evening, a staff officer brought a captured Japanese map annotated with all the American positions. Del Valle realized that the enemy already knew where the 1st Marine Division had entered the fight.

At dawn, Marines attacked into a jagged country (known as the Awacha Pocket). With all their combat expertise, Marines were no more immune to the relentless storm of shells and bullets than the soldiers they relieved. This frustrating day was a forewarning of future conditions. It rained hard as Marines secured the closest high ground. They came under such intense fire from nearby strongholds and other higher ground that they had to retreat. Dozens of Japanese infiltrators snuck up on the withdrawing Marines and engaged them in savage hand-to-hand combat. According to a Marine survivor: "That, was a bitch."

The 1st Division's veterans from Peleliu weren't strangers to cave warfare. No other division had as much practical experience. While nothing on Okinawa could match the Umurbrogol Pocket's steep cliffs, heavy vegetation, and array of fortified ridges, the "Old Breed" of the 1st Division faced a more numerous and smarter enemy. The 1st Division fought through four straight weeks of hell. The funnel created by the cliffs and draws reduced most of the Allied attacks to savage frontal assaults by fully exposed infantry/tank/engineer teams. General Buckner described this small unit fighting as: "a slugging match with temporary and limited opportunity to maneuver."

General Buckner captured the media's imagination with his "blowtorch and corkscrew" tactics needed for successful cave warfare. But to the Marine and Army veterans of Peleliu, Iwo Jima, and Biak, he was just stating the obvious—flamethrowers were the blowtorch and demolitions the corkscrew. But both weapons had to be delivered from close range by tanks and exposed infantry covering them.

On May 3, the rains finally let up, and the Marines resumed their assault. This time they took and held the first tier of vital terrain in the Awacha Pocket. But even after a methodical reduction of enemy strong points, it would take another full week of fierce fighting. Fire support proved to be an excellent asset. Now it was the Army's time to return the favor of inter-service artillery support. The 27th Division's Field Artillery Regiment stayed on the line with its forward observers and linemen familiar with the terrain.

Here, Japanese defensive discipline began to crack. General Ushijima encouraged discussion and debate from his staff regarding tactical courses of action. These heated discussions were generally between chief of staff, Lieutenant General Cho and conservative operations officer, Colonel Yahara. So far, Yahara's strategy of a "delay and bleed" holding action had prevailed. The *Thirty-second Army* had resisted the massive Allied invasion for over a month. With their Army still intact, they could continue to inflict heavy casualties on their enemies for months while massed *kamikaze* attacks wreaked havoc on the fleet.

But maintaining a sustained defense was not *Bushido* and against General Cho's code of honor and morals. He argued for a massive counterattack. Against Yahara's protests, Ushijima sided with General Cho. The great Japanese counterattack of May 4 was ill-advised and foolhardy. Manning the assault forces would forfeit Japanese coverage of the Minatoga sector and bring Ushijima's troops forward into unfamiliar territory. To deliver the mass of the fire necessary to cover the assault, Ushijima brought most of his mortars and artillery pieces into the open. He planned to use the *26th Shipping Engineer Regiment* and other elite forces in a frontal attack. At the same time, a waterborne double envelopment would alert the Allied forces to a massive counteroffensive. Yahara winced in despair.

General Cho's recklessness was now clear. Navy "Flycatcher" patrols on both coasts interdicted the first flanking attempts by Japanese raiders in slow-moving barges and canoes. On the west coast, near Kusan, the 1/1 Marines and the 3rd Armored Amphibian Battalion greeted the enemy trying to come ashore with deadly fire—killing 727. Farther down the coast, the 2/1 Marines intercepted and killed another 175, while the 1st Reconnaissance Company and the war dog platoon hunted down and destroyed the last sixty-four men hiding in the brush. The XXIV Corps took the brunt of the overland assault. They scattered the Japanese troops into small groups before ruthlessly shooting them down.

Instead of the 1st Marine Division being surrounded and annihilated per the Japanese plan—they launched their own counterattack and advanced several hundred yards. The *Thirty-second Army* took 6,000 front-line troop casualties and lost sixty pieces of artillery in this disastrous counterattack. A tearful Ushijima promised Yahara he would never again disregard his advice. Yahara was the only senior officer to survive the counterattack and described this debacle as: "the decisive action of the campaign."

General Buckner took the initiative and organized a four-division front. He tasked General Geiger to redeploy the 6th Division south from the Motobu Peninsula. General Shepherd asked Geiger to assign his Marines to the seaward flank, to continue receiving the benefit of direct naval gunfire support. Shepherd noted his division's favorable experience with fleet support throughout the northern campaign. There was also another benefit: General Shepherd would have only one nearby unit to coordinate maneuvers and fire with—the veteran 1st Marine Division.

At dawn on May 7, General Geiger reclaimed control of the 1st Marine Division and his Corps Artillery and set up his forward command post. The next day, the 22nd Marines came in to relieve the 7th Marines on the lines north of the Asa River. The 1st Division had suffered over 1,400 casualties in the last six days while trying to cover a vast front. The two Marine divisions advanced shoulder to shoulder in the west. They were greeted by heavy rains and ferocious fire as they entered the Shuri lines. The situation was dire along the front. On May 9, the 1/1 Marines assaulted Hill 60 in a spirited attack but lost their commander, Colonel James Murray, to a sniper. Later that night, the 1/5 Marines joined in savage hand-to-hand fighting against a force of sixty Japanese troops —appearing like phantoms out of the rocks.

The heavy rains delayed the 22nd Regiment's attempt to cross the Asa River. Engineers built a narrow footbridge under intermittent fire one night. Hundreds of infantry troops raced across before two enemy soldiers wearing satchel charges strapped to their chests darted into the stream and blew themselves and the bridge to pieces. Engineers spent the next night building a more stable "Baily Bridge." Allied troop reinforcements and vehicles poured across it, but the tanks had a hell of a time traversing the soft mud along the banks. Each attempt was a new adventure. But the Marines were now south of the river in force: encouraging progress on an otherwise stalemated front.

On May 10, the 5th Marines finally fought clear of the hellish Awacha Pocket, ending a week of frustration and point-blank casualties. Now it was the 7th Marines' turn to engage their own nightmarish terrain. South of their position was Dakeshi Ridge. Buckner urged his commanders to keep up the momentum and declared a general offensive along the entire front. This announcement was probably in response to the growing criticism Buckner had been receiving from the Navy and in the media for his attrition strategy.

But the rifleman's war had progressed past high-level persuasion. The assault troops knew full well what to expect—and had a good idea of what the price in blood would be.

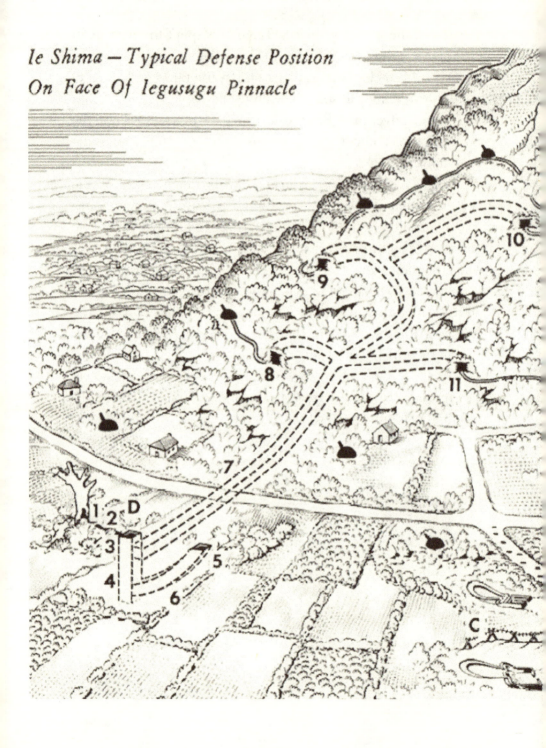

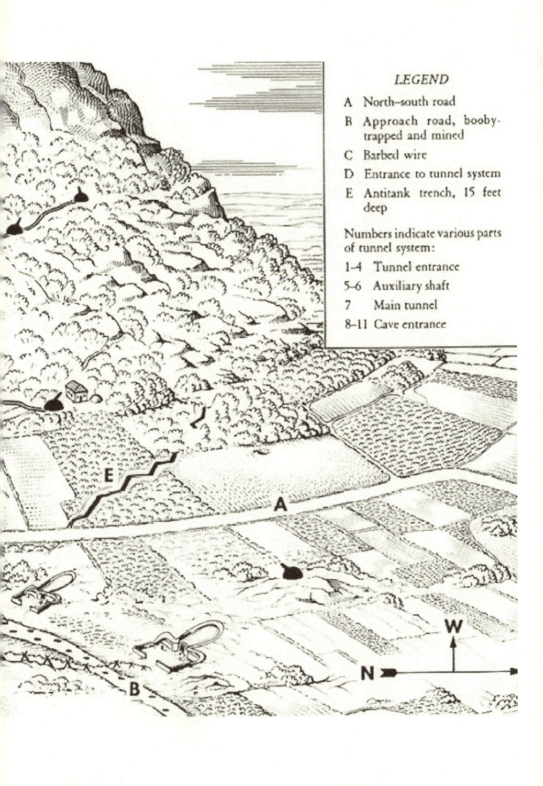

SUGAR LOAF HILL

Colonel Edward Snedeker was a veteran commander with experience fighting on Bougainville and Guadalcanal. "I was fortunate on Okinawa," Snedeker said, "in that each of my battalion commanders had fought at Peleliu. Still, our regiment had its hands full on Dakeshi Ridge. It was our most difficult mission."

After a full day of ferocious fighting, Colonel John Gormley's 1/7 Marines fought their way to Dakeshi's crest but withdrew after enemy counterattacks swarmed them like a hive of angry hornets. The next day, the 2/7 Marines retook the crest and cut down the Japanese counterattacks pouring out from the reverse slope bunkers. Now the 7th Marines were on Dakeshi to stay—another major Allied breakthrough.

The Old Breed Marines briefly celebrated this achievement before the difficulties to come dawned on them. Advancing the next 1,200 yards would take eighteen days of brutal fighting. Their most formidable obstacle would be the steep and twisted Wana Draw rambling off to the south—a lethal killing ground surrounded by towering cliffs, pockmarked with caves and mines, and covered by interlocking fire at every approach. According to General Oliver Smith: "Wana Draw was the toughest assignment the 1st Division ever encountered on Okinawa." The remains of the Japanese *62nd Infantry Division* was prepared to defend Wana to the death.

Historians have paid little attention to the 1st Division's fight against the Wana Draw defenses. Mainly because the celebrated 6th Division's assault on Sugar Loaf Hill happened at the same time. But the Wana Draw battle was just as deadly of a man-killer as the Sugar Loaf Hill battle. Colonel Arthur Mason (now leading the 1st Marine Regiment) began the assault on the Wana complex on May 12. All three infantry regiments took turns assaulting this narrow gorge to the south. The division made full use of their medium Sherman tanks and attached Army flame tanks. Both were instrumental in their assault and fire support roles. On May 16, the 1st Tank Battalion fired over 5,000 rounds of 75mm and 175,000 rounds of 30-caliber along with 650 gallons of napalm.

Crossing the gorge was a heart-stopping race through a gauntlet of enemy fire—and progress came slowly. Typical of the fighting was the division's summary for its progress on the 18th: "Gains were measured by yards won, lost, and then won again." On May 20, Colonel Stephen Sabol's 3/1 Marines improvised a new method to dislodge enemy defenders from their reverse slope positions.

In five hours of grueling, muddy work, troops manhandled several drums of napalm up to the north side of the ridge. There, Marines split the barrels open and tumbled them into the gorge, setting them on fire by dropping white phosphorus grenades in their wake. These small successes were undercut by the Japanese ability to reinforce and resupply their positions during darkness—usually screened by small-unit counter-attacks.

The close-quarters fighting was a vicious affair. General del Valle watched his casualties mount daily at an alarming rate. The 7th Marines lost 700 men taking Dakeshi and another 500 in the first five days of fighting for the Wana Draw. On May 16, Colonel E. Hunter Hurst's 3/7 Marines lost twelve officers among his rifle companies. The other regiments suffered just as terribly. From May 11-30, the division lost 200 Marines for every one hundred yards gained.

Heavy rains started again on May 22 and continued in a torrential downpour for ten days. The 1st Marine Division's sector had no roads. General del Valle committed his LVTs to deliver ammo and extract the wounded. Valle resorted to using replacements to hand-carry food and water to the front. This was not acceptable for General del Valle. He brought in torpedo bombers from Yontan Airfield and airdropped supplies by parachute. The low ceilings, heavy rain, and intense enemy fire made for hazardous duty. General del Valle did everything in his power to keep his troops supported, reinforced, supplied, and motivated—even through these grim and treacherous conditions.

To the west, the 6th Marine Division advanced south below the Asa River and collided into a trio of low hills in the open country leading to Shuri Ridge. The first of these hills was steep and unassuming (soon to be known as Sugar Loaf Hill). In the southeast was Half Moon Hill, and in the southwest was the village of Takamotoji and Horseshoe Hill. These three hills represented a singular defensive complex: the western anchor of the Shuri line.

An attack on any one of the mutually supporting defenses of these three hills would prove ineffective unless the others were simultaneously assaulted. Colonel Mita and his *15th Independent Mixed Regiment* would defend this sector to the last man. Its anti-tank guns and mortars were expertly placed to cause maximum damage to the enemy. The western slopes of Half Moon Hill had some of the most sophisticated machine-gun nests the Marines had encountered in the Pacific War. Sugar Loaf Hill had intricate, concrete-reinforced, reverse-slope positions. All approaches to this complex lay within a no-man's-land of heavy artillery from Shuri Ridge, dominating the battlefield.

Sugar Loaf Hill had an elevation of 245 feet, Half Moon at 220, and Horseshoe at 190. In comparative terms, Sugar Loaf though steep, only rose fifty feet above the northern approaches—it was no Mount Suribachi. The significance of Sugar Loaf was in the genius of the defensive fortifications and the unbridled ferocity with which the Japanese would counter-attack every US assault.

The Sugar Loaf complex was like a smaller version of Iwo Jima's Turkey Knob. As a tactical objective, Sugar Loaf lacked the physical dimensions to accommodate anything larger than a rifle company. But after eight days of fighting, that small ridge managed to chew up a handful of companies from two regiments.

Corporal James Day was a squad leader from Weapons Company 2/22. He "debatably" had the best seat in the house to watch the battle. Corporal Day's squad spent four days and three nights isolated in a shell hole in Sugar Loaf's western shoulder. On May 12, Day got orders to cross the Asa River and support Company G's attack against the small ridge. Corporal Day's squad arrived too late to do anything more than cover the fighting withdrawal of G Company. His company lost half their number in the all-day assault, including their gutsy commander, Captain Owen Stebbins (shot in both legs by a Japanese machine gunner). Corporal Day later wrote that Stebbins was: "a brave man whose tactical plan for assaulting Sugar Loaf became the pattern for all successive units to follow."

Concerned about unrestricted fire from the Half Moon Hill area, Major Henry Courtney, battalion XO, took Corporal Day and his squad with him. They moved out on the morning of May 13 on a dangerous trek to reach the 29th Marines and coordinate the upcoming assault. The 29th Marines were then committed to protecting the 2/22 Marines' left flank. Courtney tasked Corporal Day and his squad to support Company F in the following day's assault.

Day's rifle company comprised seven Marines. On the 14th, they joined Company F's assault on Sugar Loaf Hill and scampered up the left shoulder. Day got orders to backtrack his squad around the hill and take up defensive positions on the right western shoulder—this was not easy. By late afternoon Company F had been driven off their exposed left shoulder, leaving Corporal Day with just two of his squad mates in a large shell hole on the opposite shoulder.

That evening, Major Courtney led forty-five volunteers from George and Fox Companies up the left shoulder of Sugar Loaf. In a frantic battle of close-quarters fighting, the Japanese killed Major Courtney and half of his force. According to Corporal Day: "We didn't know who they were. Even though they were only fifty yards away, they were on the opposite side of the crest, we were out of visual contact. But we knew they were Marines, and we knew they were in trouble. We did our part by shooting and grenading every Jap we saw moving in their direction."

Then, Corporal Day heard the sounds of Courtney's force getting evacuated from the hill and knew they were alone on Sugar Loaf. Nineteen-year-old Corporal Day's biggest concern was letting the other Marines know where they were and replenishing their ammo and grenades. "Before dawn, I went back down the hill and there were a couple of LVTs trying to deliver critical supplies to the folks who made it through the earlier penetration. But both had been knocked out just north of the hill. I was able to raid those disabled vehicles several times for ammo, rations, and grenades. We were fine."

On May 15, Corporal Day and his men watched another Marine attack come from the northeast. This time Marines on the eastern crest of the hill were fully exposed to raking fire from the mortars on Half Moon and Horseshoe Hills. Corporal Day's Marines directed their rifle fire into a column of enemy troops running toward Sugar Loaf from Horseshoe: "we really needed a machine gun."

But good fortune provided them with a 30-caliber air-cooled M1919A4 left behind in the wake of the withdrawing Marines. Day's gunner put the weapon into action on the forward parapet of their hole. But an enemy 47mm crew opened up from Horseshoe Hill, killing the Marine gunner and destroying the gun. Now there were only two riflemen left on the ridgetop.

DAY AND BERTOLI

On May 15, tragedy struck the 1/22 Marines. A crushing Japanese bombardment caught the command group assembled at their observation post while they planned their next attack. Shellfire killed the CO, Major Tom Myers. Every other company commander was wounded, including the CO and XO of the supporting tank company. General Shepherd wrote: "it was the greatest single loss the division had sustained. Major Myers was an outstanding leader."

Major Earl Cook, the battalion XO, took command and continued to make assault preparations. Division staff released a warning: "The enemy is able to accurately locate our OPs and CPs because of the commanding ground he occupies. The dangerous practice of permitting unnecessary crowding exposure in these areas will have serious consequences."

That warning was worthless. Commanders had to observe the action to command. Exposure to interdictive fire was a risk you had to take as an infantry battalion commander. The following day, Colonel Jean Moreau, CO of the 1/29 Marines, suffered a serious wound when an enemy shell hit his observation post. His XO, Major Robert Neuffer, took over, and the battle raged on.

According to Corporal Day's last surviving squad mate, Private First Class Dale Bertoli: "The Japs were the only ones up there, and they gave us their full attention. While we had plenty of grenades and ammo, it was still pretty hairy."

Sugar Loaf Hill's south slope was the steepest. Japanese troops swarmed from their caves on the reverse slopes but had a tough climb to get at the Marines on the ridge. Day and Bertoli greeted enemy troops scrambling up the rocks with grenades. The Japanese troops who survived this mini-barrage were backlit by flares as they struggled over and back down the ridge. Day and Bertoli were back to back in the dark side of the crater—an excellent position to shoot down fleeing Japanese troops.

According to Corporal Day: "I believed that Sugar Loaf would fall on the 16th. We looked back and down and saw the battle shaping up. A great panorama." The two squad mates hunkered down while artillery, mortars, and tanks hammered the ridge. Day saw the fire coming from the enemy had not slackened: "Sugar Loaf's real danger wasn't the hill where we were, it was a 300-yard kill zone the Marines had to cross to approach the hill from the north. It was a grim sight. Men falling, tanks getting knocked out . . . division must've suffered over 600 casualties in that one day." Looking back, the 6th Marine Division considered May 16 to be the bloodiest day of the entire campaign.

The battered 22nd Marines were down to forty percent effectiveness. General Shepherd relieved them with the 29th and installed fresh regimental leadership, replacing the CO and XO with Colonels Harold Roberts and August Larson. When the weather cleared during the late afternoon on the 16th, Day and Bertoli could see well past Horseshoe Hill and all the way to the Asato River. Steady columns of Japanese reinforcements surged northward through Takamotoji village and toward the battlefield. Day and Bertoli kept firing at them from 600 yards away, keeping a small but persistent thorn in the enemy's defenses. Their rifle fire drew substantial attention from crawling squads of nighttime enemy raiders.

Corporal Day recalled: "They came at us from 2045 and on all night. All we could do was to keep tossing grenades and firing at them with our M-1s. Marines north of Sugar Loaf tried to help us with mortar fire, but it came a little too close, and both me and Bertoli were wounded by shrapnel and burned by white phosphorus."

At dawn on the 17th, a runner from the 29th Marines

scrambled up to their shell-pocked crater with orders to "get the hell out of there." A massive naval, air, and artillery bombardment was underway. Day and Bertoli did not hesitate. They were exhausted and partially deaf, but still had the energy to stumble back down the hill to safety. Day and Bertoli endured a series of debriefings from staff officers, while a roaring bombardment crashed down on the three hills.

May 17 was the fifth day of battle for Sugar Loaf Hill. It was 2/29 Easy Company's turn to attack the complex's defenses. While brave and persistent, Easy Company's several assaults fared little better than their predecessors. During one of these ferocious attacks, the 29th Marines reported to division: "E Company moved to the top of the ridge and had thirty men south of Sugar Loaf. [E Co.] sustained two close-in charges and killed a hell of a lot of Nips. Moving back to base to reform and at dusk, we are going again, We will take it."

But Sugar Loaf did not fall. At dusk, after overcoming another savage onslaught of bayonets, flashing knives, and hand-to-hand combat against a brutal counterattack, Easy Company withdrew—taking 160 casualties.

May 18 marked the beginning of incessant rain. In this soupy mess, Dog Company, 2/29 Marines, attacked Sugar Loaf Hill. They were supported by tanks that braved the minefields on both shoulders of Sugar Loaf to penetrate the no-man's-land just to the south. When the enemy swarmed out of their reverse-slope caves for another counterattack—tanks destroyed them. Dog Company earned the honor of becoming the first rifle company to hold Sugar Loaf overnight. Marines would not give up that bloody and costly ground.

The shot-up and exhausted 29th Marines still needed to take Half Moon and Horseshoe Hills. General Geiger adjusted the tactical boundaries westward and brought the 1st

Marine Division into the fight for Horseshoe Hill. Geiger also released the 4th Marines from Corps reserve.

General Shepherd deployed the fresh Marines into the battle on the 19th. The battle raged, and the 4th Marines took seventy casualties just relieving the 29th Marines. But with Sugar Loaf now in Allied hands, the battle's momentum shifted. On May 20, Colonel Reynolds Hayden's 1/4 Marines (with help from the 2/4 and 3/4) made notable gains on both flanks. By the end of the day, Marines had secured Half Moon Hill and a good portion of Horseshoe.

Enemy reinforcements funneled into the fight from the southwest. The Marines prepared for nighttime visitors at Horseshoe Hill. Japanese troops came in massive numbers: 700 sailors and soldiers smashing into Marine defenders throughout much of the night. Colonel Bruno Hochmuth's 3/4 Marines had six artillery battalions in direct support of the attack and fifteen battalions at the height of the fighting. Throughout the crisis on Horseshoe, Hochmuth kept in radio contact with Colonel Bruce Hemphill, who commanded the support artillery battalions.

This exchange between commanders reduced the number of short rounds and allowed Marines to provide accurate fire on the Japanese. This hellish rain of shells blew massive holes into the ranks of every Japanese advance: Marine riflemen met those who survived with their bayonets. The enemy counter attackers died to the man.

The victory at Sugar Loaf lacked a climactic finish. There was no celebration ceremony here. The sniper-infested ruins of Naha loomed ahead, with Shuri Ridge in the distance. The 1st Marine Division sidestepped the last of the Wana defenses to the east. The 6th Marine Division crept west while the 4th Marines crossed the chest-high Asa River on May 23. The III

Amphibious Corps stood primed on the outskirts of Okinawa's capital city.

* * *

The Army's XXIV Corps matched the Marines' breakthroughs and success. On the east coast, the 96th Division secured Conical Hill (opposite Sugar Loaf on the Shuri anchor line) after weeks of fierce fighting. On May 22, the 7th secured Yonabaru.

Now, the Japanese Thirty-*second Army* faced a real risk of being cut off from both flanks. General Ushijima (this time) took Colonel Yahara's advice. Instead of fighting to the death at Shuri Castle, the remaining Japanese troops took advantage of the awful weather. They streamed southward to their last line of prepared defenses in the Kiyamu Peninsula. General Ushijima masterfully executed this maneuver. While Allied pilots spotted and interdicted the southbound columns, they reported other columns moving north. General Buckner believed the Japanese were rotating units in defense of Shuri. But these northbound troops were ragtag units tasked with a suicide rearguard action. At this, they succeeded.

On May 29, a South Carolina company commander raised the "Stars and Bars" Confederate flag over the abandoned Shuri Castle. According to General del Valle: "every damn OP that could see that flag started telephoning me and raising Cain. I had one hell of a hullabaloo on the telephone. I agreed to replace that rebel flag with the Stars and Stripes, but it took two days to get it through the Japs rear guards."

On May 31, Colonel Richard Ross, CO of the 3/1 Marines, raised the Stars and Stripes over Shuri Castle and then took cover. Unlike Sugar Loaf Hill, Shuri Castle could be seen from all over southern Okinawa. Every Japanese gunner within range opened up on the hated American colors. Even though the Stars & Stripes fluttered over Shuri Castle, and the formidable enemy defenses had been breached, the Japanese *Thirty-second Army* still remained as deadly a fighting force as ever. The enemy would sell their lives dearly for the final eight shell-pocked, rain-soaked miles of southern Okinawa.

SCREAMING MIMI

Withdrawing Japanese troops did not easily escape from their Shuri defenses. US Navy spotter planes found the southbound column and called in a devastating fire from every available attack craft and half a dozen ships.

Soon after, many miles of that muddy road were littered with wrecked field guns, trucks, and corpses. General del Valle congratulated the Tactical Air Force: "Thanks for the prompt response this afternoon when the Nips were caught on the road with their kimonos down."

Still, most of General Ushijima's *Thirty-second Army* survived and made it to their "Alamo" on the Kiyamu Peninsula. The Tenth Army missed an opportunity to end the battle a month early—stalled by heavy rains and deep mud—simply too encumbered to swiftly respond.

Allied infantry trudged south, cursing the weather but glad to be past the Shuri line. Every advance exacted a price in blood. A Japanese sniper killed Colonel Horatio Woodhouse, CO of the 2/22 Marines (and General Shepherd's cousin) as he led his battalion toward the Kokuba Estuary. Shepherd grieved privately at the loss of his young cousin and put the battalion XO, Colonel John G. Johnson, in command.

As troops of the III Amphibious Corps continued south, Marines came upon a series of east-west ridges that dominated open farmlands. Colonel Snedeker wrote: "The southern part of Okinawa consisted primarily of cross ridges that stuck out like the bones of a fish." In the meantime, divisions from the Army's XXIV Corps carefully approached the towering escarpments in their zone. The remaining Japanese troops had gone to ground again along the ridges and peaks—lying in wait to ambush the Allied advance.

Rain and mud plagued the advancing Allied forces. In Eugene Sledge's book, he described this battlefield as a "five-mile sea of mud." PFC Sledge wrote: "The mud in camp on

Pavuvu was a nuisance. But the mud on that Okinawan battlefield was misery beyond description."

The 96th Division reported the results of a full day's efforts under these conditions: "those on the reverse slope slid back and those on the forward slope down—otherwise no change."

Marines chafed at the heavy-handed controls of the Tenth Army, which seemed to stall at each encounter with a Japanese outpost. General Buckner preferred a massive application of firepower and destroying every obstacle before committing troops into the open. Colonel Shapley, CO of the 4th Marines, disagreed: "I'm not too sure that sometimes when they whittle you away, ten to twelve men a day, that maybe it would be better to take a hundred losses a day to get out sooner."

Colonel Wilburt "Bigfoot," Brown, CO of the 11th Marines (legendary veteran artilleryman) believed the Tenth Army relied too heavily on firepower. "We dumped a tremendous amount of metal into those Jap positions. Nothing could have lived through that churning mass of roaring and falling shells—but when we advanced, the Nips were still there—and mad as hell." Colonel Brown also had strong feelings about the overuse of star shells for night illumination: "It was like we were the children of Israel in the wilderness: living under a pillar of fire by night and a cloud of smoke by day."

This heavy reliance on artillery support stressed the amphibious supply system. The Tenth Army's demand for heavy ordinance grew to over 3,000 tons of ammunition per day. Each round had to be delivered to the beach and distributed along the front. This reduced the availability of other supplies, including rations. Frontline troops began to go hungry. Partial support came from the friendly skies when Marine torpedo-bombers air-dropped rations during the first three days of June.

Offshore, the fleet endured waves of *kamikaze* attacks. On

May 17, Admiral Turner announced an end to the amphibious assault phase and departed. General Buckner now reported to Admiral Spruance. Admiral Harry Hill assumed command of the enormous amphibious force still supporting the Tenth Army. On May 27, Admiral "Bull" Halsey relieved Spruance. And the Fifth Fleet officially became the Third Fleet: same crew, same ships, different designation. Turner and Spruance began plotting their next amphibious assault—Operation Downfall—the invasion of the Japanese home islands.

General Shepherd appreciated the vast amphibious resources available and decided to inject some tactical mobility into this sluggish campaign. For the 6th Division to secure the Naha Airfield, Shepherd had to first overcome the Oroku Peninsula. The hard way of achieving this would be to attack from the peninsula's base and scratch seaward. Or Shepherd could launch a shore-to-shore amphibious assault and surprise the enemy on their flank. "The Japanese expected us to cross the Kokuba," Shepherd said. "I wanted to surprise them."

Shepherd convinced General Geiger of the wisdom of this approach, but getting General Buckner's approval took much longer. Eventually, Buckner agreed but only gave the 6th Marine Division thirty-six hours to plan and execute this division-level amphibious assault.

Colonel Krulak relished this challenge. Scouts from Major "Cold Steel" Walker's 6th Recon Company crept across the statuary at night to gather intelligence on the enemy defenders and Nishikoku Beaches. Scouts confirmed a cobbled force of Japanese Navy units under an old adversary. The final opposed amphibious landing of the Pacific War would be launched against one of the last surviving SNLF (Special Naval Landing Force) commanders—Admiral Minoru Ota.

Admiral Ota was fifty-four years old and a graduate of the

Japanese Naval Academy. A veteran of the elite SNLF service from as early as 1932 in Shanghai. Ten years later, he commanded the *2nd Combined Special Landing Force* meant to assault Midway but was prevented by the catastrophic naval defeat suffered by the Japanese.

In November 1942, he commanded the *8th Combined Special Landing Force* in the Solomons, defending Bairoko against the 1st Marine Raiders. By 1945, the SNLF had mostly disappeared. Ota was in command of a motley outfit of several thousand coastal defense and antiaircraft gunners, aviation mechanics, and construction specialists. Ota still breathed fire into his forces. He equipped his ragtag troops with hundreds of machine cannons from wrecked aircraft and made them sow thousands of mines.

Shepherd knew he was in for a fight and that he faced a skilled opponent; he also realized that he had the advantage of surprise if his forces could act quickly. The final planning details centered on problems with the division's previously dependable LVTs. The hard-fighting onshore had taken a hefty toll on the tracks and suspension systems of these amphibious assault vehicles—and there were no repair parts available. Worse, the first typhoon of the season was approaching, and the Navy was getting jumpy. General Shepherd remained resolute in executing the assault on June 4, and Admiral Halsey backed him up.

Shepherd chose Colonel Shapley to lead the 4th Marines in the assault. Shapley divided the 650-yard Nishikoku Beach between the 1/4 Marines on the right and the 2/4 on the left. Despite the heavy rains, the assault jumped off on schedule. The Oroku Peninsula exploded in smoke and flame under the hammering of hundreds of naval guns, aerial bombs, and artillery batteries. Scouts secured Ono Yama island while the 4th Marines swept across the statuary. LCIs and LCMs loaded with tanks appeared from Loomis Harbor in the north.

The amphibious force achieved total surprise. Many of the busted-up LVTs broke down en route, causing delays, but enemy fire was negligible. Empty LVTs from the first waves quickly returned to rescue the stranded troops. The 4th Marines rapidly advanced with Colonel Whaling's 29th Marines close behind. By dusk, Marines occupied 1,200 yards on Oroku Peninsula. A furious Admiral Ota redeployed his sailors to the threat from the rear.

This amphibious assault had been near-perfect and a model for future study in amphib ops. The typhoon blew through while the Marines occupied the peninsula and captured the airfield in two days. On June 7, when the 1st Division reached the southwest coast north of Itoman, Admiral Ota's force had no chance of escape. General Shepherd ordered a threefold enveloping movement with his regiments—leading to the inevitable outcome.

The battle for the Oroku Peninsula was savage. Admiral Ota was no ordinary enemy commander. His 5,000 troops fought with a warrior's spirit and were heavily armed. No similar size Okinawan force had so many automatic weapons or so effectively placed mines. Marines encountered devastating enemy weapons at short range—rail-mounted 8-inch rockets, "the Screaming Mimi," and massive 320mm spigot mortars firing "Flying Ashcans."

On June 9, the 4th Marines reported: "Stubborn defense of high ground by MG and 20mm fire. Character of opposition unchanged. L Hill under attack from two sides. Another tank shot on right flank, thinking 8-inch gun."

Admiral Ota saw the end coming. On June 6, he reported to Tokyo: "The troops have fought valiantly in the finest tradition of the Japanese Navy. While fierce bombardments may have deformed the mountains of Okinawa, they cannot alter the loyal spirit of our men." Three days later, Ota sent his final message to General Ushijima: "Enemy tank groups now attack our cave headquarters. The naval force will have a glorious death." Ota committed ritual suicide—his duty now done.

General Shepherd had defeated a competent and worthy foe. In his Oroku operation after-action report he said: "In ten days of fighting we killed 5,000 Japanese and took 200 prisoners. Mines disabled thirty of our tanks. One tank was destroyed by two direct hits from an 8-inch naval gun at point-blank range. 1,608 Marines were wounded or killed."

WRAPPING UP THE FIGHT

When the 1st Marine Division reached the coast near Itoman, it was the first time the division had access to the sea in over a month. This relieved the veteran division's extended supply lines. Colonel Snedeker, CO of the 7th Marines, wrote: "As we reached the shore we were helped a great deal by amphibian tractors that had come down the coast with supplies. Otherwise, there was no way in hell we could get supplies overland."

The wide-open southern country allowed General del Valle to further refine the deployment of his infantry-tank teams. No unit in the Tenth Army surpassed the 1st Marine Division's synchronization of these two supporting arms. Using those painfully learned tactical lessons from Peleliu, the 1st Division never allowed their tanks to range beyond the support of accompanying artillery and infantry. This resulted in the 1st Tank Battalion being the only armored unit in the battle not to lose a tank to Japanese suicide squads—even during the swirling close-quarter combat at Wana Draw.

General del Valle appreciated his attached Army 4.2

mortar battery: "My tanks had such good luck because the 4.2s were vital in Okinawa. We developed the tank infantry training to a fare-thee-well in those swales—backed up by the 4.2-inch mortars."

According to Colonel "Bigfoot" Brown of the 11th Marines: "Working with Lieutenant Colonel 'Jeb' Stuart and the 1st Tank Battalion, we developed a new method of protecting tanks and reducing infantry vulnerability during the assault. We'd put an artillery observer in one of those tanks with a radio to one of the 155mm howitzer battalions. We used both packs of the 75mm, and LVT-As with the airburst capabilities. If any Jap [suicider] showed his face anywhere, we opened fire with an airburst and kept a pattern of pattering shell fragments around the tanks."

On June 10, Colonel Jim Magee's 2/1 Marines used similar tactics in a bloody all-day assault on Hill 69—west of Ozato. Magee's Marines lost three tanks to enemy artillery in the approach. But they still took the hill and held it through a savage enemy counterattack that night.

Kunishi Ridge loomed beyond Hill 69. A steep coral escarpment dominated the surrounding grasslands and rice patties. Kunishi was longer and higher than Sugar Loaf, but equally honeycombed with enemy caves and tunnels. While it lacked cover with Half-Moon and Horseshoe on its rear flanks, it was still protected from behind by Masato Ridge—500 yards south. Fragments of the veteran *32nd Infantry Regiment* defended the many hidden bunkers. This was the last of General Ushijima's organized frontline troops. Kunishi Ridge would be as deadly a killing ground as the Marines would ever face in the Pacific War.

On June 11, enemy gunners repelled the first tank-infantry assaults by the 7th Marines. Colonel Snedeker had a different plan: "I realized, due to the losses of experienced leadership, we'd never be able to take Kunishi Ridge in the daytime. I thought a night attack could be successful."

Snedeker flew over his objective and devised his plan. Tenth Army night assaults were rare in this campaign—especially Snedeker's ambitious plan of deploying two battalions. But General del Valle approved his plan, and at 0330 the next morning, the 1/7 and 2/7 departed the combat outpost for the dark ridge. By 0500, lead companies of both battalions swarmed over the crest and surprised several enemy groups calmly cooking breakfast. Then, a brutal battle to expand the toehold on the ridge exploded into action.

As dawn broke, enemy gunners targeted relief infantry columns as Marines clung to the crest and endured showers of shrapnel from grenades and mortar rounds. According to General del Valle: "This situation was one of the tactical oddities in this type of peculiar warfare. We were *on* the ridge, and the Japs were *in* the ridge, on both the forward and reverse slopes."

Marines on Kunishi desperately needed supplies and reinforcements. The growing number of wounded needed evacuation. Only the medium Shermans had the bulk and the ability to provide relief. Over the next several days, the 1st Tank Battalion (even losing twenty-two Shermans to enemy fire) made remarkable achievements. They removed two crewmen to make room for six replacement riflemen inside each tank. Once on top of the hill they exchanged replacements for wounded, but no one could stand without getting shot. So, all the exchanges had to take place through the escape hatch in the bottom of the tanks.

This became a familiar sight on Kunishi Ridge: a buttoned-up tank lurching up to besieged Marine positions while replacements slithered out via the escape hatch carrying ammo, rations, water, and plasma. Then, other Marines crawled under the Shermans, dragging their wounded on ponchos—manhandling them through the small escape hatch. For those severely wounded, they had the unsavory privilege of riding down to safety lashed topside behind the turret. Tank drivers provided maximum protection to their exposed stretcher cases by backing down the entire 850-yard gauntlet. In this meticulous way, tankers delivered fifty fresh troops and evacuated thirty-five wounded men the day after the 7th Marines' night assault.

General del Valle was pleased with these results and ordered Colonel Mason to execute a similar night assault in the 1st Marine sector of Kunishi Ridge. This mission went to the 2/1 Marines, who accomplished it on the night of June 13 despite careless lapses of illumination fire by forgetful supporting arms.

Furious Japanese swarmed out of their bunkers in a massive counterattack. Losses mounted quickly in Colonel Magee's ranks. One company lost six of seven officers that morning, before the 1st Tank Battalion came to the rescue delivering reinforcements and evacuating 110 wounded Marines by nightfall.

General del Valle wrote: "The Japs were so damn surprised. They used to counterattack us at night all the time. I bet they never felt we'd have the audacity to go out and do it to them."

During Colonel Yahara's interrogation, he admitted the Marine night attacks effectively caught his troops off-guard—psychologically and physically.

By June 15, the 1st Marines had been fighting for twelve straight days: sustaining 500 casualties. The 5th Marines replaced them with an elaborate nighttime relief on June 15.

The 1st Marines, back in the safety of division reserve, received their newest orders: *If not otherwise occupied, you will bury Japs in your area.*

The battle for Kunishi Ridge raged. PFC Sledge approached the embattled escarpment with dread. He later wrote: "That crest looked so much like Bloody Nose that my knees nearly buckled. I felt like I was back on Peleliu and had to go through that hell all over again." The fighting along that crest and its slopes took place at point-blank range—even for Sledge's 60mm mortars. His crew then became stretcher-bearers in this highly hazardous duty. Half of his company was wounded within the next twenty-two hours.

Getting wounded Marines off Kunishi Ridge was no easy task. The seriously wounded needed to endure another half day of evacuation by field ambulance over bad roads and enemy fire. Then, pilots stepped in with a great idea. Engineers cleared a rough landing strip suitable for "Grasshopper" observation aircraft. Corpsmen hustled to deliver casualties from Kunishi and Hill 69 to the crude airfield. They were gently loaded into waiting "Piper Cubs" and flown back to the field hospitals in the rear—an eight-minute flight. This was the dawn of tactical medevacs, which saved so many lives in the subsequent Asian wars. Marine pilots flew out 640 casualties in eleven days: saving countless lives.

The 6th Marine Division joined the southern battlefield after securing the Oroku Peninsula. The *32nd Infantry Regiment* died a hard death after the combined forces of III Amphibious Corps swept north and overlapped Mezado Ridge and could smell the sea along the south coast. In Ira Saki, Marines from Company G (2/22) raised the 6th Division's colors on the island's southernmost point.

The long-neglected 2nd Marine Division finally got into the fight in the closing week of the campaign. Colonel Clarence Wallace and his 8th Marines arrived from Saipan to capture the two outlying islands—Aguni Shima and Iheya Shima—this would give the fleet more early warning radar sites against *kamikaze* raids. Colonel Wallace commanded a considerable force (essentially a brigade), including the 2/10 Marines and the 2nd Amphibian Tractor Battalion. General Geiger assigned the 8th Marines to the 1st Division, and on June 18, they relieved the 7th Marines and swept southeast with ferocity.

PFC Sledge recalled the arrival of the 8th Marines: "We scrutinized these Marines with the hard professional stare of old salts sizing up another outfit. Everything we saw brought forth remarks of approval."

General Buckner was interested in observing the 8th Marines' first combat deployment. Earlier, he'd been impressed with Colonel Wallace's outfit during an inspection visit to Saipan. Buckner went to a forward observation post on June 18 to watch the 8th Marines advance along the valley floor. Enemy gunners on the opposite ridge saw the official party and opened up. A shell struck a close coral outcrop and drove a lethal splinter into the general's chest. Buckner died in ten minutes. One of the few senior American officers killed in action in World War II.

General Geiger assumed command. His third star became effective immediately. The Tenth Army was in capable hands. Geiger became the only Marine—and the only pilot of any service—to command a field army. The Okinawan soldiers had no qualms about this. Senior Army echelons elsewhere did. Army General Joseph Stillwell received urgent orders to Okinawa. Five days later, he relieved Geiger. But by then, the battle was over.

When news of General Buckner's death reached the *Thirty-second Army* headquarters in its cliff-side cave near Mabuni—the enemy officers cheered—but General Ushijima remained silent. He respected Buckner's military ancestry and appreciated that they'd both once commanded their respective service academies: Buckner at West Point and Ushijima at Zama.

Ushijima knew his end was approaching fast. The 7th and 96th Divisions were nearly on top of Japanese command. On June 21, General Ushijima ordered his men to "save themselves so they could tell the story to Army headquarters." Then he committed *Seppuku*. Ushijima plunged his *Tantō* (short knife) into his belly, drawing the blade from left to right before Colonel Yahara shot him in the back of the head—Ushijima collapsed into a pool of his own blood.

General Geiger declared the end of organized resistance on Okinawa the same day. True to form, a final *kamikaze* attack struck the fleet that night, and sharp fighting broke out on the 22nd. Undeterred, General Geiger ordered the 2nd Marine Aircraft Wing in action and ran up the American flag at Tenth Army headquarters.

The long battle was finally over.

GENERAL ROY GEIGER

Marine commanders on Okinawa were well-versed and seasoned combat veterans of joint service operations. These qualities contributed to the ultimate victory of the US Tenth Army.

General Roy Geiger was a 60-year-old native of Middleburg, Florida. He graduated from Florida State and Stetson University law schools before commanding III Amphibious Corps. He enlisted in the Marines in 1907 and became a naval aviator (the fifth Marine ever) in 1917.

Geiger flew combat missions in World War I France and commanded a squadron of the Northern Bombing Group. In 1942 on Guadalcanal, he commanded the 1st Marine Aircraft Wing. The following year, he took command of the 1st Marine Amphibious Corps on Bougainville for the invasion of Guam and the Palaus.

Geiger knew combat. Even on Okinawa, he made frequent visits to the front lines of combat outposts. On two separate occasions, he "appropriated" an observation plane to fly over the battlefield for his own personal reconnaissance.

After the death of General Buckner, Geiger took command of the Tenth Army and was immediately promoted to lieutenant general. Geiger also relieved General Holland Smith as commanding general of the Fleet Marine Force Pacific. Geiger was one of the few Marines invited to attend the Tokyo Bay Japanese surrender ceremony on the USS *Missouri*, September 2, 1945.

Geiger was an observer at the 1946 atomic bomb tests at Bikini Lagoon. His solemn evaluation of the vulnerability of future surface ship-to-shore assaults of atomic munitions spurred the Marine Corps to develop the transport helicopter. General Geiger died from lung cancer in 1947.

GENERAL PEDRO DEL VALLE

General Pedro del Valle commanded the 1st Marine Division. He was a 51-year-old native of San Juan, Puerto Rico. In 1915 he graduated from the Naval Academy. He commanded a Marine detachment on board the battleship *Texas* in the North Atlantic during World War I.

Years of expeditionary campaigns and sea duty in the Caribbean and Central America gave del Valle a vision of how Marines could better serve the Navy and their country at war. In 1931, General Randolph Berkeley appointed del Valle (then a major) to the "Landing Operations Board" in Quantico. This was the first organizational step taken by the Marine Corps to develop a working doctrine for amphibious assaults.

In February 1932, he published a provocative essay about ship to shore amphibious operations in the *Marine Corps Gazette*. He challenged his fellow officers to think seriously of executing an opposed landing.

A decade later, del Valle (now a veteran artilleryman) commanded the 11th Marines with distinction during the

Guadalcanal campaign. Many surviving Japanese admired the superb artillery of the Marines. Following that, del Valle commanded corps artillery for III Amphibious Corps long before assuming command of the "Old Breed" on Okinawa. General del Valle died in 1978 at the age of 84.

GENERAL LEMUEL SHEPHERD JR.

General Lemuel Shepherd Jr. was a 49-year-old native of Norfolk, Virginia. He graduated from the Virginia Military Institute in 1917 and served with distinction with the 5th Marines in France. He was wounded three times and received the Navy Cross. Shepherd became one of those rare infantry officers who'd commanded every possible echelon from division all the way down to rifle platoon. Early in the Pacific, he commanded the 9th Marines and served as assistant commander of the 1st Marine Division at Cape Gloucester before taking command of the 1st Provisional Marine Brigade on Guam.

In September 1944, Shepherd became the first commanding general of the newly formed 6th Marine Division and served with honor on Okinawa. After the war, he commanded the Fleet Marine Force Pacific for the first two years of the Korean War. In 1952, he became the 20th Commandant of the Marine Corps. General Shepherd died at age 94 from bone cancer in La Jolla, California.

GENERAL FRANCIS MULCAHY

General Francis Mulcahy commanded the Tenth Army Tactical Air Force. He was a 51-year-old native of Rochester, New York, and graduated from Notre Dame before his commission in 1917. He attended naval flight school the same year, and like Roy Geiger, Mulcahy flew bombing missions in World War I France. He pioneered the Marine Corps' close air support and ground operations in the interwar years of expeditionary campaigns in Central America and the Caribbean.

After the attack on Pearl Harbor, Mulcahy served as an observer with the British Western Desert Air Force in North Africa. When he deployed to the Pacific, he took command of the 2nd Marine Aircraft Wing. In the final months of the Guadalcanal campaign, Mulcahy served with distinction in command of all Allied Air Forces in the Solomons. Mulcahy worked meticulously at the airfields on Yontan and Kadena to coordinate combat deployments against the *kamikaze* threats to the fleet.

General Mulcahy received three Distinguished Service

Medals for his heroic accomplishments in France, the Solomons, and Okinawa before his death in 1973.

BLOOD AND IRON

Army infantry and Marines faced fierce opposition from over 100,000 enemy troops under the command of General Ushijima. Allied intelligence originally estimated Ushijima's *Thirty-second Army* strength at 65,000. But many other reinforcing organizations traveled to Okinawa from previous posts on Manchuria, China, and Japan.

The *9th Infantry Division* was the first to arrive. They were an elite veteran unit—the backbone of Ushijima's defense forces. Following them was the *44th Independent Mixed Brigade* (which lost part of their strength when one of their ships was torpedoed). The *15th Independent Mixed Regiment* was flown to Okinawa and added to the remains of the *44th*. The next large unit was the *24th Infantry Division*, coming from Manchuria. They were well-trained and equipped, but had not yet been bloodied in battle. The final major infantry unit to arrive was General Fujioka's *62nd Infantry Division* comprising two brigades of four independent infantry battalions.

Imperial Japanese headquarters saw the battle of Okinawa as a fixed defensive fight. Other than the *27th Tank Regiment*, Ushijima was not given any strong armored force. Japanese headquarters diverted large weapon shipments and troops to Okinawa because of the hopeless situation in the Philippines and their inability to deliver reinforcements and supplies. The *Thirty-second Army* possessed a heavier concentration of artillery under a single command than had been available to other Japanese commanders anywhere else in the Pacific War.

Total Japanese artillery strength was grouped into the *5th Artillery Command*. General Wada's command comprised two independent artillery regiments and artillery elements of the *44th Brigade* and the *27th Tank Regiment*. He also had thirty-six howitzers and eight 150mm guns with the *1st* and *2nd Medium Artillery Regiment*.

Wada also had the *1st Independent Heavy Mortar Regiment* firing the 320mm spigot mortars first encountered by Marines on Iwo Jima. Their ninety-six 81mm mortars were assigned for close infantry support and controlled by sector defense commanders.

Potential infantry replacements varied from excellent with the *26th Shipping Engineer Regiment* to meager at best with the various rear area service units. The *10th Air Sector Command* provided 7,000 replacements composed of airfield maintenance and construction units at the Kadena and Yontan Airfields. Seven sea-raiding squadrons based at Kerama Retto had one-hundred handpicked men whose only assignment was to smash explosive-loaded suicide craft into the sides of cargo vessels and assault transports.

A native Okinawan home guard (called *Boeitai*) rounded out the *Thirty-second Army*. These men were trained and integrated into Army units. The *Boeitai* gave Ushijima another 20,000 extra men to use as he pleased. Add to this 1,700 Okinawan children (thirteen years old and up) organized into volunteer youth groups called "Blood and Iron" for the Emperor's duty units.

US ARMY TROOPS

The US Army played a significant role in the victory on Okinawa. The Army deployed as many combat troops, suffered comparable casualties, and fought with an equal heroism and bravery as the Marines.

Army battles for Conical Hill, Kakazu Ridge, and the escarpment at Yuza Dake were just as bloody and memorable as Nishi Ridge and Sugar Loaf for the Marines. The Okinawa campaign still serves today as a model of joint service cooperation despite its isolated cases of sibling rivalry.

In mid-1943, the Joint Chiefs identified three divisions in the Pacific with amphibious "proficiency." The 1st and 2nd Marine Divisions were veterans of Tulagi and Guadalcanal, while the 7th Infantry was fresh from fighting in the Aleutians. These three units joined with four other divisions and constituted the Tenth Army bound for Okinawa. The number of divisions with experience in amphibious operations in the Pacific had now expanded sevenfold.

Three assault units in General John Hodge's XXIV Corps had recent experience with amphibious landings in the Battle for Leyte Gulf. It was the 96th Division's first campaign and the third amphibious operation for the 7th Division after Kwajalein and Attu. The veteran 77th Division executed a daring landing at Ormoc, which surprised and slaughtered the enemy defenders.

The 27th was a National Guard unit still bitterly regarded by Marines after their flail on Saipan, but still a proud unit with amphibious experience in the Marianas and Gilbert Islands. No other army divisions had the luxury of extended preparations for Okinawa. General MacArthur didn't release the underfed and under-strength XXIV Corps (after 112 days of combat on Leyte) to the Tenth Army until seven weeks before L-Day on Okinawa. The 27th Division had more time but endured inadequate training in the jungles of Espiritu Santo.

There were many examples of Marines and Army units

cooperating in the Okinawan campaign. Army Air Force P-47 Thunderbolts flew long-range bombing and fighter missions for General Mulcahy's Tactical Air Force. Army and Marine Corps units supported opposite services regularly during the long drive to the Shuri line. Marines gained a healthy respect for the Army's 8-inch howitzers. These heavy weapons were often the only way to breach a well-fortified enemy strong point.

General Buckner attached deadly "Zippo tanks" from the 713th Armored Flame Thrower Battalion along with 4.2-inch mortar batteries to both Marine divisions. The 6th Marine Division also had the 708th Amphibian Tank Battalion attached for the entire battle. Each of these units received a Presidential Unit Citation for service with their parent Marine units.

The Army often gave logistical support to the Marines as the campaign slogged south during the endless rains. The Marines' fourth revision of their table of organization still did not provide enough transfer assets to support such a lengthy campaign conducted far from the forces' beachhead. A shortage of amphibious cargo ships assigned to the Marines also reduced the number of LVTs and wheeled logistics vehicles available. Often, the generosity of the supporting Army units determined if the Marines would eat that day.

An example of this cooperative spirit happened on June 4, when soldiers from the 96th Division gave rations to Colonel Richard Ross's starving and exhausted Marines. This brightened the battalion on a day otherwise known as "the most miserable day spent on Okinawa."

In short, Okinawa was too difficult and too large for one service to undertake. In this eighty-two-day campaign against a well-armed, resolute enemy, victory required teamwork and cooperation from several services.

MARINES AVIATION UNITS

According to Colonel Vernon McGee, landing force air support commander during the battle: "Okinawa was the culmination of the development of air support doctrine in the Pacific. The procedures we used there were results of all lessons learned in preceding campaigns—including the Philippines."

Marine aviation units on Okinawa operated across a range of missions: from bombing enemy battleships to supply drops.

Over 700 Marine planes took part in the Okinawa campaign. An estimated 450 of these were engaged in combat for half the battle. Most Marine air units served under the Tenth Army's TAF (Tactical Air Force) commanded by General Mulcahy. Outside of the TAF, Marine fighter squadrons were assigned to fleet carriers or escort carriers and long-range transports.

Admiral Spruance commanded all Allied forces for Operation Iceberg. He believed the enemy's air arm was the biggest threat to the mission's success. Spruance made the Tenth Army's first objective to secure the Kadena and Yontan Airfields and support land-based fighter squadrons.

Assault forces achieve this on L-Day. The next day, General Mulcahy moved his command post ashore and began TAF operations. His top priority was to maintain air superiority over Okinawa and the Fifth Fleet. Because of the massed *kamikaze* attacks unleashed by the Japanese, this mission kept Mulcahy preoccupied for many weeks.

Army and Marine aviation units composed Mulcahy's Tactical Air Force. His force had fifteen Marine fighter squadrons, ten Army fighter squadrons, two Marine torpedo bomber squadrons, and sixteen Army bomber squadrons. Marine fighter pilots flew F4U Corsairs and radar-equipped, night-fighting F6F Hellcats. Army pilots flew P-47 Thunderbolts, and their night fighters were P-61 Black Widows.

Allied pilots fought air-to-air duels against *kamikazes* and plenty of other late-model "Franks" and "Jacks." Altogether, the Tactical Air Force pilots shot down 627 planes. Colonel Ward Dickey's Marine Aircraft Group (MAG-33) set the record with 215 kills—more than half claimed by the "Death Rattlers"—Major George Axtell's squadron VMF-323.

The need to protect the Fleet caused some ground

commanders to worry that their own close-in air support would be "short-sheeted." But escort carrier Naval squadrons picked up the slack. They flew over sixty percent of the close-in support missions between April 1 and the end of June. The combined TAF and carrier pilots flew over 14,000 air support sorties. Over 5,000 of these supported Marines on the ground. Pilots dropped over 150,000 gallons of napalm on enemy positions.

Air Liaison Parties accompanied the frontline divisions and directed aircraft to the target. Coordinating these lower echelon requests became the responsibility of three Marine Landing Force Air Support Control Units. One represented the Tenth Army to the fleet while the others were responsive to IIIAC and the XXIV Corps. This technique refined experiments McGee had started on Iwo Jima. In most cases, close air support for the infantry was extremely effective. Several units reported safe and prompt delivery of ordnance on target within 150 yards. But there were also accidents and delays (less than a dozen) and situations where lines were simply too intermingled for any air support.

Other Marine aviation units helped in the victory on Okinawa. Marine torpedo bomber pilots flew their Avenger "torpeckers" in zero-zero weather. They dropped over 40,000 pounds of medical supplies, rations, and ammunition to forward-deployed ground units. The fragile and small Grasshoppers of the Marine Observation Squadrons flew 3,487 missions of artillery spotting, medical evacuations, and photo-reconnaissance. One artillery officer described the Grasshopper pilots as: "the unsung heroes of Marine aviation. They'd often fly past cave openings and look in to see if the Japs were hiding a gun in there."

Marine pilots served on Okinawa with panache. During a

desperate dogfight, one pilot radioed: "Come on up here and help me. I got two Franks, and a Zeke cornered." Those were his last words, but his fighting spirit persisted. According to a destroyer skipper who'd just been rescued from swarms of *kamikazes* by Marine Corsairs: "I'd take my ship to the shores of Japan if I could have those Marines with me."

ARTILLERY ON OKINAWA

Because of the tactics selected and the nature of enemy defenses, Okinawa was the most significant battle in the war for artillery units. General Geiger landed with fourteen firing battalions with the IIIAC. And when the 2/10 Marines came ashore to support the 8th Marines—the total rose to fifteen firing battalions.

General David Nimmer commanded the III Corps

Artillery with three batteries of 155mm howitzers and three 155mm "Long Tom" guns. The Marines had considerably enhanced their firepower since the initial Pacific campaigns.

While one 75mm howitzer battalion still remained, the 105mm howitzer had become the norm for division artillery. Infantry units on the front line were supported by the 75mm fire of medium tanks and LVT-As. New self-propelled "siege guns" with 4.5-inch multiple rocket launchers fired by the "Buck Rogers" men and attached Army 4.2 mortar platoons caused chaos on Japanese positions.

Colonel Fred Henderson described this devastating array of fire support: "Not many people realize that the Tenth Army's artillery, plus the LVT-As and naval gunfire gave us a guns/mile of front ratio on Okinawa that was higher than any US effort in all of World War II."

General Buckner tasked his commanders to integrate field artillery support early in the campaign. General Geiger sent his corps artillery and 11th Marines (not fully committed in the opening weeks) to help the XXIV Army Corps in their early assaults against the outer Shuri defenses. From April 7 to May 6, these artillery units fired over 55,000 rounds in support of the XXIV Corps. But this was only the beginning. Once both IIIAC Marine divisions entered the lines, they benefited from Army artillery support and organic fire support—two Marine and two Army.

By the end, the Tenth Army artillery rockets had fired over two million rounds downrange. In addition, 707,000 mortars, rockets, and five-inch or larger shells were fired from naval gunfire ships offshore. Half of the artillery rounds were from 105mm howitzer shells and the M-7 self-propelled guns. Compared to these bigger guns, the older 75mm pack howitzers were the battlefield's "Tiny Tims." Their versatility and mobility proved valuable through the long haul.

Operation Iceberg

According to Colonel Brown, who commanded the LVT-As firing similar ammunition: "The 75mm was plentiful and contrasted with the heavy calibers, so we used it for fire interdiction and harassing missions across the front."

Generals del Valle and Geiger expressed interest in the army's larger weapons. Geiger respected the Army's 8-inch howitzer 200-pound shell. It had much more penetrating and destroying power than the 155mm gun's ninety-five-pound shell—largest in the Marine's inventory. Geiger urged Marine Corps Headquarters to form 8-inch howitzer battalions for the next attack on Japan. Geiger also praised the accuracy, range, and power of the Army's 4.2-inch mortars, and recommended their inclusion in the Marine division.

On several occasions, artillery commanders were tempted to orchestrate all this killing power into one mighty concentrated attack. Time on target (TOT) missions frequently occurred in the early weeks, but their high consumption rates were a drawback. Late in the campaign, Colonel Brown coordinated a massive TOT with twenty-two battalions against enemy positions in southern Okinawa. This sudden concentration worked brilliantly, but Brown failed to inform the generals and woke everyone from a sound sleep. Brown "caught hell" from all sides.

Geiger insisted the LVT-As were also trained as field artillery. While this was done, the opportunity for direct fire support in the assault waves fizzled on L-Day when the enemy chose to not defend the Hagushi breaches. Colonel Lewis Metzger's 1st Armored Amphibian Battalion LVT-As fired over 20,000 rounds of 75mm shells in an artillery support role after L-Day.

Marines made great advances in refining supporting arms coordination during the battle for Okinawa. Commanders established Target Information Centers (TIC) at every level from battalion up to Tenth Army. The TICs provided centralized target information and a weapons assignment system responsive to both assigned targets and targets of opportunity. All three component liaison officers: air, artillery, and naval gunfire, were staffed with target intelligence information officers.

This commitment to innovation led to significant support improvements for the foot-slogging infantry. As one rifle battalion commander later wrote: "It wasn't uncommon for a battleship, artillery, tanks, and aircraft to be supporting the efforts of a single platoon during the assault on Shuri."

SHERMAN M-4 TANKS

Seven Marine and Army tank battalions were deployed on Okinawa. They were a deadly weapon—but only when coordinated with accompanying infantry. The Japanese tried to separate the two components by boldness and fire.

Before the invasion, General Ushijima said: "The strength of the enemy's forces is with his tanks." Ushijima's anti-tank training received the highest priority within his *Thirty-second Army*. These preparations proved successful on April 19, when the Japanese knocked out twenty-two out of the thirty Sherman tanks of the 27th Division—mostly by suicidal demolitionists.

The Marines fared better. They learned in earlier campaigns how to integrate artillery and infantry in a close protective over-watch of their tanks and to keep the "human bullet" suicide squads at bay. While enemy mines and guns took their toll on the Shermans, only one Marine tank sustained damage from a Japanese suicide attack.

Colonel Arthur Stewart commanded the 1st Tank Battalion on Okinawa. His unit had fought with distinction at Peleliu six months earlier, despite shipping shortfalls that kept a third of his tanks out of the fight. Stewart insisted on keeping the battalion's older M-4A2 Shermans because their twin (General Motors) diesel engines were safer in combat: "The tanks were not so easily set on fire and blown up under enemy fire," Stewart wrote after the war.

Colonel Rob Denig preferred the newer Sherman model M-4A3 for his 6th Tank Battalion. Denig's tank crews liked the greater horsepower provided by the water-cooled Ford V-8 engines. They considered the reversion to gasoline from diesel an acceptable risk. The 6th Tank Battalion faced its greatest challenge against Admiral Ota's naval guns and mines on the Oroku Peninsula.

Sherman tanks were harshly criticized in the European

theater for coming up short against the heavier German Tiger Tanks. But they were ideal for island fighting in the Pacific. On Okinawa, the Sherman's limitations were obvious. Their 75mm gun was too light against most of Ushijima's fortifications. But the new M-7 self-propelled 155mm gun worked well. Shermans were never known for their armor protection. At thirty-three tons, their strength was more in mobility and reliability. Japanese anti-tank weapons and mines reached the height of their deadliness on Okinawa. The Sherman's thin-skinned weak points (1.5-inch armor on the rear and sides) caused considerable concern.

Marine tank crews sheathed the sides of their tanks with lumber to thwart hand-lobbed Japanese magnetic mines as early as the Marshalls. By Okinawa, the Shermans were draped with spot-welded track blocks, sandbags, wire mesh, and clusters of large nails—designed to enhance armor protection.

Both tank battalions had their Shermans configured with dozer blades (valuable for cave fighting), but neither deployed with flame tanks. Despite the rave reports of the USN Mark I turret-mounted flame system installed on the Shermans in the Iwo Jima battle, there was no retrofit program for the Okinawa-bound Marine tank units. All flame tanks on Okinawa were provided courtesy of the US Army's 713th Armored Flamethrower Battalion. Company B of that unit supported the Marines with three brand-new H1 flame tanks. Each carried 290 gallons of napalm thickened fuel—good for two-and-a-half minutes of flame at a range of 200 yards.

Marines used the new T-6 "tank flotation devices" to get the initial waves of Shermans ashore on L-Day. The T-6 was a series of floating tanks welded around the hull. They had a provisional steering device that made use of the tracks and electric bilge pumps. Once ashore, the crew jettisoned the bulky rig with built-in explosive charges.

The April 1 landing for the 1st Tank Battalion was truly "April Fool's Day." An LST (Landing Ship Tank) captain carrying six Shermans equipped with a T-6 launched the vehicles an hour late and eleven miles out to sea. It took them five hours to reach the beach (losing two tanks on the reef at ebb tide). Most of Colonel Stewart's other Shermans made it ashore before noon, but some of his reserves could not make it across the reef for another forty-eight hours.

The Sixth Tank Battalion had better luck. Their LST skippers launched their T-6 tanks on time and close in. Two tanks were lost: one sank after its main engine failed, and the other broke a track and swerved into a hole. The other Shermans surged ashore and were ready to roll.

Enemy gunners and mine warfare experts knocked out three Marine Shermans in the battle. Many more tanks took damage from the fighting but were repaired by the hardworking maintenance crews. Because of their ingenuity, the assault infantry battalions never lacked armored firepower, shock action, and mobility.

AMPHIBIOUS RECONNAISSANCE

A series of smaller amphibious operations around the periphery of Okinawa helped contribute to victory. These landing forces varied in size from the company level to an entire division. Each reflected the apex of amphibious expertise learned in the Pacific theater by 1945. These landings produced fleet anchorages, auxiliary airfields, fire support bases, and expeditionary radar sites, giving an early warning to the fleet against the dreaded *kamikazes*.

The Amphibious Reconnaissance Battalion commanded by Major James Jones provided outstanding service to landing force commanders in a series of audacious exploits in the Marianas, Marshalls, Gilberts, and on Iwo Jima. Before L-Day on Okinawa, these Marines supported the Army's 77th Division with stealthy landings on Awara Saki, Keise Shima, and other islands in the East China Sea. Later in the battle, this recon unit executed night landings on the islands guarding the eastern approaches to Nakagusuku Wan (later known as Buckner Bay).

On one of those islands—Tsugen Jima, the main Japanese outpost—Jones and his recon Marines had a ferocious firefight before he could extract his men through the darkness. The Army's 105th Infantry stormed ashore on Tsugen Jima three days later and eliminated the stronghold and all resistance. On April 13, Jones' Marines then sailed northwest and executed a night landing on Minna Shima to seize a firebase supporting the 77th's main landing on Ie Shima.

The post-L-Day amphibious operations with the 27th and 77th Divisions were helpful—but not decisive. By mid-April, the Tenth Army had waged a campaign of massive firepower against the primary Japanese defenses. General Buckner chose not to employ amphibious resources to break the gridlock. Buckner's long deliberation of whether to use the "amphib card" was not helped by a lack of flexibility by the Joint Chiefs, who kept strings attached to the use of the Marine divisions. The Japanese *Thirty-second Army* in southern Okinawa was the enemy's center of gravity in the Ryukyu Islands. But still, the

Joint Chiefs let weeks pass before scrubbing earlier commitments to send the 2nd Marine Division into attack Kikai Shima—an obscure island north of Okinawa.

General Buckner used the 8th Marines in a pair of amphibious landings on June 3 to seize outlying islands for early warning radar facilities against the *kamikaze* raids. Then, the commanding general attached the reinforced regiment to the 1st Marine Division for the final overland assaults on the south.

Buckner consented to the 6th Marine Division's request to conduct its own amphibious assault below Naha to surprise the Naval Guard Force on the Oroku Peninsula. This was a jewel of an operation in which the Marines used every component of amphibious warfare to their great advantage.

If the 77th Division's amphibious landings on Ie Shima or the 6th Marine Division's landing on Oroku had been executed separately from the Okinawan campaign, they would both have received major historical study for the size of forces, brilliant orchestration, and intensity of the fighting.

While both operations provided valuable objectives: unrestricted access to Naha's ports and Ie Shima airfields. They were only secondary to the more extensive campaign and barely received a passing mention. The Oroku operation would be the final unopposed amphibious landing of the war.

LEGACY OF OKINAWA

The exhausted Marines on Okinawa showed little joy at the official proclamation of victory. The death throes of the *Thirty-second Army* kept the battlefield deadly. The last of General

Ushijima's infantry may have died defending Yuza Dake and Kunishi Ridge, but the remaining mishmash of support troops sold their lives dearly to the last man.

On June 18, diehard enemy survivors wounded Major Earl Cook, CO of the 1/22 Marines, and Colonel Hunter Hurst, CO of the 3/7. Even Day and Bertoli, who'd survived so long in that crater on Sugar Loaf, watched their luck run out in the final days. Private First Class Bertoli died in action. Corporal Day was seriously wounded by a satchel charge and required urgent evacuation to the hospital ship *Solace*.

The butcher's bill on Okinawa was costly to both sides. Over 120,000 Japanese died defending the island, while 7,000 surrendered at the end. The native Okinawans suffered the worst. Recent studies show that over 150,000 civilians died in the fighting—one-third of the island's population. The Tenth Army suffered over 45,000 combat casualties, including 7,264 dead Americans. An additional 26,000 nonviolent casualties were incurred: primarily cases of combat fatigue.

The Marine Corps' overall casualties: air, ship detachments, and ground were 19,821. In addition, 562 members of the Navy Medical Corps were wounded or killed. General Shepherd described the corpsmen on Okinawa as: "the finest and most courageous men that I'd ever known. They did a magnificent job."

Losses within the infantry (as usual) were disproportionate with other Allied outfits. Colonel Shapley reported his losses as 110 percent in the 4th Marines. This number represents the replacements and their high attrition in the battle. Corporal Day of the 2/22 Marines experienced the death of his battalion and regimental commanders, plus the killing and wounding of his two company commanders, seven platoon commanders, and every other member of his rifle squad.

The legacy of this epic battle can be defined through the following points:

Foreshadow to the Invasion of Japan

Admiral Spruance described the Okinawan battle as: "the bloody and hellish prelude to the invasion of Japan." As wicked a nightmare as Okinawa was, every survivor knew the subsequent battles on Honshu and Kyushu would be worse. The operational plans for invading Japan specified the use of surviving veterans from Iwo Jima and Luzon. The reward for the Okinawan survivors would be to land on the main island of Honshu. Most of the men were fatalistic—no man's luck could last through those hellish infernos.

Mastery of amphibious tactics

The massive and nearly flawless amphibious assault on Okinawa happened thirty years (to the month) after the disaster at Gallipoli in World War I. By 1945, the Allied forces had refined this difficult naval mission into an art form. Admiral Nimitz had every advantage in place for Okinawa: specialized ships and landing craft, a proven doctrine, mission-oriented weapons systems, flexible logistics, trained shock troops, and unity of command. Everything clicked and everything worked. The projection (and execution) of 60,000 combat troops landed ashore on L-Day validated an amphibious doctrine earlier considered suicidal.

Attrition style warfare

Ignoring the great opportunities for maneuver and surprise available in the amphibious task force, the Tenth Army executed most assaults on Okinawa using an unimaginative attrition style of warfare, which played to the Japanese defenders' strength. This unrealistic reliance on firepower and siege tactics only prolonged the fighting. The Oroku Peninsula and Ie Shima Landings (despite being successful) comprise the only division-level amphibious assaults after L-Day. Also, the few night attacks made in unison by the Army and Marine forces (which were successful) were not encouraged. The Tenth Army squandered several opportunities for tactical innovations that could have hastened a breakthrough into enemy defenses.

Unity of service

Excluding squabbles between the 77th Infantry Division and 1st Marine Division after the Marines' seizure of Shuri Castle (in the Army's zone), the battle for Okinawa represented joint service cooperation at its finest. This was General Buckner's finest achievement, and General Geiger continued with this level of teamwork after Buckner was impaled through the chest and killed in action. The battle of Okinawa today is still a model of study in inter-service cooperation for succeeding generations of military professionals.

The best training

Marines deployed in Okinawa received the most practical and thoroughly advanced training of the war. Well-seasoned and battle-hardened division and regimental commanders anticipated Okinawa's requirements for cave warfare. They built-up areas to conduct realistic rehearsals and training. This battle produced few surprises.

Many Marines who survived Okinawa went on to top positions of leadership that influenced the Marine Corps for the next two decades. Two Marine Corps commandants emerged from this hellish ordeal: General Lemuel Shepherd of the 6th Marine Division and Colonel Leonard Chapman, CO of the 4/11 Marines. Oliver Smith and Vernon McGee were promoted to the rank of four-star general. At least seventeen others achieved the rank of lieutenant general—including George Axtell, Alan Shapley, Ed Snedeker, and Victor Krulak.

Corporal James Day recovered from his wounds and returned to Okinawa forty years later as a Major General in command of all Marine Corps bases on the island.

During the taping of the battle's fiftieth anniversary, General Victor Krulak gave a fitting epitaph to the brave men who gave their lives on Okinawa. Speaking on camera, he said: "The cheerfulness with which they went to their death has stayed with me forever. What is it that makes them all the same? I watched them in Korea, I watched them in Vietnam, and it's the same. American youth is one hell of a lot better than he is usually credited."

***

Building a relationship with my readers is one of the best things about writing. I occasionally send out emails with details on new releases and special offers. If you'd like to join my free readers group and never miss a new release, just tap here and I'll add you to the list.

ALSO BY DANIEL WRINN

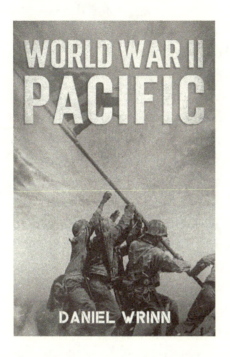

WORLD WAR II PACIFIC: BATTLES AND CAMPAIGNS FROM GUADALCANAL TO OKINAWA 1942-1945

"A brisk and compelling game changer for the historiography of the Pacific Theater in World War II." – Reader

An enlightening glimpse into nine battles and campaigns during the Pacific War Allied offensive.

Each of these momentous operations were fascinating feats of strategy, planning, and bravery, handing the Allies what would eventually become a victory over the Pacific Theater and an end to Imperialist Japanese expansion.

Operation Watchtower, a riveting exploration of the spark that set off the Allied offensive in the Pacific islands, detailing the grueling struggle for the island of Guadalcanal and its vital strategic position.

Operation Galvanic, an incredible account of the battle for the Tarawa Atoll and base that would give them a steppingstone into the heart of Japanese-controlled waters.

Operation Backhander, a gripping retelling of the war for Cape Gloucester, New Guinea, and the Bismarck Sea.

Battle for Saipan, Marines stormed the beaches with a goal of gaining a crucial air base from which the US could launch its new long-range B-29 bombers directly at Japan's home islands.

Invasion of Tinian, is the incredible account of the assault on Tinian. Located just under six miles southwest of Saipan. This was the first use of napalm and the "shore to shore" concept.

Recapture of Guam, a gripping narrative about the liberation of the Japanese-held island of Guam, captured by the Japanese in 1941 during one of the first Pacific campaigns of the War.

Operation Stalemate, Marines landed on the island of Peleliu, one of the Palau Islands in the Pacific, as part of a larger operation to provide support for General MacArthur, who was preparing to invade the Philippines.

Operation Detachment, the battle of Iwo Jima was a major offensive in World War II. The Marine invasion was tasked with the mission of capturing airfields on the island for use by P-51 fighters.

Operation Iceberg, the invasion and ultimate victory on Okinawa was the largest amphibious assault in the Pacific Theater. It was also one of the bloodiest battles in the Pacific, lasting ninety-eight days.

This gripping narrative sheds light on these often-overlooked facets of WWII, providing students, history fans, and World War II buffs alike with a captivating breakdown of the history and combat that defined the ultimate victory of US forces in the Pacific.

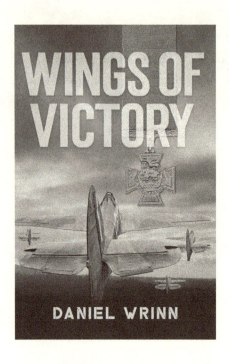

Wings of Victory: World War II adventures in a war-torn Europe

"Historical fiction with a realistic twist." – Reviewer

Thrilling World War II adventures like you've never seen them before.

As the Nazis invade Europe on a campaign for total domination, a brutal war begins to unfold which will change the course of the world forever—and John Archer finds himself caught in the middle of it. When this amateur pilot joins the Allied war effort and is tasked with a series of death-defying missions which place him deep into German-occupied territory, his hair-raising adventures will help decide the fate of Europe.

In **War Heroes**, John is caught up in the devastating Nazi invasion of France while on vacation. Teaming up with ambulance driver Barney, John will need his amateur pilot skills and more than a stroke of luck to pull off the escape of the century.

In **Bombs Over Britain**, the Nazis have a plan which could change the course of the entire war . . . unless Archer can stop them. Air-dropped into Belgium on a top-secret mission, Archer must retrieve vital intelligence and make it out alive. But that's easier said than done when the Gestapo are closing in.

And in **Desert Scout**, Archer finds himself stranded beneath the scorching Libyan sun and in a race against time to turn the tide of the war in North Africa. But with the Luftwaffe and the desert vying to finish him off, can he make it out alive?

Packed with action and filled to the brim with suspense, these thrilling stories combine classic adventures with a riveting and historical World War II setting, making it ideal for history buffs and casual readers. If you're a fan of riveting war fiction novels, WW2 aircraft, and the war for the skies, Archer's next adventure will keep you on the edge of your seat.

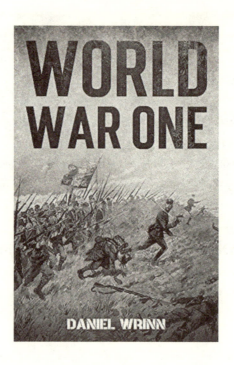

World War One: WWI History told from the Trenches, Seas, Skies, and Desert of a War Torn World

"Compelling . . . the kind of book that brings history alive." – Reviewer

Dive into the incredible history of WWI with these gripping stories.

With a unique and fascinating glimpse into the lesser-known stories of the War to End All Wars, this riveting book unveils four thrilling stories from the trenches, seas, skies, and desert of a war-torn world. From one captain's death-defying mission to smuggle weapons for an Irish rebellion to heroic pilots and soldiers from all corners of the globe, these stories shed light on real people and events from one of the greatest conflicts in human history.

• **WWI: Tales from the Trenches**, a sweeping and eerily realistic narrative which explores the struggles and endless dangers faced by soldiers in the trenches during the heart of WWI

• **Broken Wings**, a powerful and heroic story about one pilot after he was shot down and spent 72 harrowing days on the run deep behind enemy lines

• **Mission to Ireland**, which explores the devious and cunning plan to smuggle a ship loaded with weapons to incite an Irish rebellion against the British

• And **Journey into Eden**, a fascinating glimpse into the lesser-known battles on the harsh and unforgiving Mesopotamian Front

World War I reduced Europe's mightiest empires to rubble, killed twenty million people, and cracked the foundations of our modern world. In its wake, empires toppled, monarchies fell, and whole populations lost their national identities.

Each of these stories brings together unbelievable real-life WWI history, making them perfect for casual readers and history buffs alike. If you want to peer into the past and unearth the incredible stories of the brave soldiers who risked everything, then this book is for you.

REFERENCES

Alexander, Joseph H. *The Final Campaign: Marines in the Victory on Okinawa*. Washington, D.C.: Marine Corps Historical Center, 1996.

Appleman, Roy Edgar, James Burns, Russel Gugeler, and Stevens John. *Okinawa: The Last Battle*. Washington: United States Army Center of Military History, 1948.

Fisch, Arnold G. *Ryukyus*. Washington, D.C.: U.S. Army Center of Military History, 2004.

Hastings, Max. *Retribution: The Battle for Japan, 1944-45*. New York: Alfred A. Knopf, 2007.

Hobbs, David. *The British Pacific Fleet: the Royal Navy's Most Powerful Strike Force*. Barnsley, South Yorkshire: Seaforth Publishing, 2012.

References

Lacey, Laura Homan. *Stay Off the Skyline: The Sixth Marine Division on Okinawa: an Oral History*. Potomac Books, 2005.

Manchester, William. *Goodbye Darkness*. Boston, Mass: Little, Brown and Co., 1980.

Morison, Samuel Eliot. *Victory in the Pacific, 1945 Vol. 14 of History of United States Naval Operations in World War II*. Urbana: University of Illinois Press, 2002.

Nash, Douglas. *Battle of Okinawa III MEF Staff Ride Battle Book*. U.S. Marine Corps History Division, 2015.

Nichols, Chas S., and Henry I. Shaw. *Okinawa: Victory in the Pacific (PDF)*. Washington, D.C.: Government Printing Office, 1955.

Rottman, Gordon L. *Okinawa, 1945: the Last Battle*. Oxford: Osprey Pub., 2002.

Sledge, E. B., and Paul Fussell. *With the Old Breed At Peleliu and Okinawa*. New York: Oxford University Press, 1991.

World War 2 Pictures. "Okinawa Pictures." WW2-Pictures.com, April 16, 2010.

ABOUT THE AUTHOR

Daniel Wrinn writes Military History & War Stories. A US Navy veteran and avid history buff, Daniel lives in the Utah Wasatch Mountains. He writes every day with a view of the snow capped peaks of Park City to keep him company. You can join his readers group and get notified of new releases, special offers, and free books here:

www.danielwrinn.com

Copyright © 2021 by Daniel Wrinn

All rights reserved.

No part of this book may be reproduced in any form or by any electronic or mechanical means, including information storage and retrieval systems, without written permission from the author, except for the use of brief quotations in a book review.

CPSIA information can be obtained
at www.ICGtesting.com
Printed in the USA
BVHW030806071221
623421BV00011B/48